Missionaries

The Rural African Village Adventure

Reverend John Paul Emmanuel

Valentine Publishing House
Denver, Colorado

This is a work of fiction. The names, characters, dialogues, incidents, places and events portrayed in this book are the product of the author's imagination and are used fictitiously. Any resemblance to actual events or persons, living or dead, including businesses, companies or locations is entirely coincidental.

The Scripture passages contained herein are quoted from the character's memory and are based on the *New Revised Standard Version Bible*, copyright © 1989 by the Division of Christian Education of the National Council of the Churches of Christ in the U.S.A. Used by permission. All rights reserved.

For more information about special discounts or bulk purchases, please contact Valentine Publishing House at 1-877-266-5289.

Publisher's Cataloging-in-Publication Data
    Missionaries / Reverend John Paul Emmanuel.
    Volume Three / The Rural African Village Adventure.

    p. cm.
    LCCN: 2023951972
    ISBN-10: 0-9994908-3-4
    ISBN-13: 978-0-9994908-3-9

    1. Christian Fiction.
    2. Spiritual Warfare.
    3. Evangelization.

    PS3562.A315R44 2024
    813'.54–dc22
    2023951972

Printed in the United States of America.

"Do you not know that in a race the runners all compete, but only one receives the prize? Run in such a way that you may win it. Athletes exercise self-control in all things; they do it to receive a perishable wreath, but we an imperishable one. So I do not run aimlessly, nor do I box as though beating the air; but I punish my body and enslave it, so that after proclaiming to others I myself should not be disqualified."

1 Corinthians 9:24–27

1st CHAPTER

After the missionaries prayed for Amber's recovery, Overwatch sent an assignment of ministering angels that descended upon the intensive care unit at Lakeside Regional Hospital.

When the demonic spirits realized that God's angelic army had arrived, several demons fled through the exterior walls of the building, but they were hunted down and destroyed before they could return to Narco-Leóna's base of operations. The remaining demonic spirits that had wrapped their tentacles around Amber's head and shoulders needed to be supernaturally removed. Once all the demonic spirits had been destroyed, Amber began breathing on her own.

As the missionaries were leaving the intensive care unit at the hospital, Michelle said, "I'm so happy that we're fasting this week. I feel so much closer to the Lord. Fasting not only gives me a deeper contemplative hunger for God's Word, but it also intensifies my awareness of the Holy Spirit's presence. I could feel such a profound sense of peace when we were praying for Amber, that I think she's going to be okay."

"I still think we need to come back tomorrow and continue praying for her recovery," Matthew said.

Because the demonic spirits that had been assigned to eliminate Amber never returned to report on their progress, Narco-Leóna summoned a shadow-stalking spirit named Draven and said, "Go to the hospital and check on the execution. Make sure the feather-neck is dead, and then find a way to stop those monkeys."

When Draven arrived at Lakeside Regional Hospital, he disguised his appearance and entered into the air filtration system so that he could approach the intensive care unit without being detected. After slowly maneuvering through a series of air ducts, he was able to discern that Amber's bedside was surrounded by a team of ministering angels, so he returned to Narco-Leóna and said, "There's no sign of our assault force. They were all destroyed in the battle, and the monkeys are still on the loose. They have been praying for the feather-neck's recovery."

"I want you to stay extremely close to the male baboon," Narco-Leóna said. "Follow him around day and night. Come up with a strategy for his destruction."

After the missionaries made several more visits to the hospital, Amber regained consciousness late one evening and began fighting with the nurses. She wanted the intravenous tubes that were connected to her arms, along with the feeding tube that had been installed through her abdomen, removed so she could go back to her life on the streets.

Because the feeding tube needed to remain for several more weeks, the nurses gave Amber heavy doses of sedatives so the hospital counselor and chaplain could help her make a full recovery.

On the fifth day of the fast, Michelle stopped by Matthew's apartment to share the good news. She sat down at the kitchen table and said, "Monica at the Metropolitan Art Gallery loved the idea of hosting a homeless fundraising event. I began my presentation by showing her some of my favorite signs, 'Seeking Human Kindness' and 'Need Cash for Alcohol Research.' After I unfolded the large sign that said, 'I stand here humiliated, but it beats committing a crime,' she agreed to host the event for a ten percent commission."

"That's great news," Matthew said.

"The only drawback is that her schedule is extremely busy for the next several months," Michelle said. "The only opening was a Friday evening in June."

"That seems so far away," Matthew said.

"I know you have been waiting a long time for this moment to arrive, but the extra time will give us the opportunity to collect a few more signs at the Rescue Mission," Michelle said. "In addition, we could use the extra time to properly advertise the event. I would like to invite Chaplain Hemingway and all of his friends, along with all of Monica's business associates. We also need to invite the parents of our Jclub members and all of our Christian Singles International members."

"The longer wait time may be a blessing in disguise," Matthew said. "The lease on my apartment expires at the end of July, so I was thinking about moving everything into storage and parking my truck at your mom's house."

Because Michelle didn't respond to the proposal, Matthew said, "I know that look. What's wrong?"

"I'm sure my mom would be happy to watch over your truck while we're traveling, but don't you think we are moving a little too fast?" Michelle asked. "A few days ago, you didn't know what country to visit in Africa, and now you want to move the contents of your apartment into storage."

"I know it sounds a little extreme, but ever since we started fasting, I have been asking the Lord simple yes-or-no questions about the direction of my life," Matthew said. "During my contemplative time with the Lord, I have been meditating on those questions, and I have been receiving an abundance of crystal-clear answers."

"What kind of questions have you been asking the Lord?" Michelle asked.

"Before I show you the map of Africa and take you through the entire process, can I offer you some juice?" Matthew asked. "I have been experimenting with a new juice using pie pumpkins, and I think you might like it."

"I didn't know there was any juice in a pie pump-kin," Michelle said.

"I never bought pie pumpkins before," Matthew said, "but because the supermarket was selling them at a discount, I purchased several and baked them in the oven like an acorn squash.

"To make pie pumpkin juice, all you need to do is heat the pulp in boiling water and then put the mixture in the blender with an apple and a little cinnamon. It makes a thick and sweet juice, which has been perfect during the evening."

After Matthew finished making two glasses of pumpkin juice, he showed Michelle a map of Africa and said, "I started by researching the safest countries in Africa. Then I eliminated all the countries that didn't speak English as their official language. I was able to narrow the list down to three countries: Ghana, Tanzania and Liberia. I wanted to visit Madagascar because it's home to those little ring-tailed lemurs that you like, but they speak French."

"I know how to speak a little French, and those lemurs are so cute," Michelle said.

"Madagascar is on the top of our list of places to visit in Africa, but I'm feeling called to work with the Muslims in Kenya," Matthew said.

"Why Kenya?" Michelle asked.

"It's not the safest country in Africa, but they speak English as their official language, and it's a major ministry hub for many of the surrounding regions," Matthew said. "There are a lot of international flights that fly into Nairobi, so the airfare prices will be lower."

"I'm assuming they also have a high Muslim population," Michelle said.

"There's a lot more Christians in Kenya than Muslims," Matthew said. "According to government statistics, only eleven percent of the country is Muslim, twenty percent is Catholic, and over fifty percent of the residents self-identify as either protestant or evangelical. There's also a high percentage of native African religions throughout the region."[1]

"Do you have any ministry connections that can be trusted in Kenya?" Michelle asked.

"I have been working on that," Matthew said. "We basically have three choices: One option is to make friends with some of the people who have sent unsolicited emails through our ministry website begging for money. This is probably the worst option because of all the scams that originate in Africa, but I have already made contact with two pastors from Kenya this way. Pastor Emeka sounds like he has an authentic church, and the other man sounds like an Internet cafe scammer."

"How can you tell the difference between a real pastor and a scammer?" Michelle asked.

"A scammer will spend all of his time on the Internet begging for money," Matthew said. "He will usually start an email conversation needing Bibles for his so-called church, and then he will only want the money to buy the Bibles, because he doesn't want them delivered by the International Bible Society. Once you send this man a small amount of money, a major tragedy will occur and he will need even more money. A real pastor will not have time to write and respond to several email messages per day, because he is way too busy taking care of his flock."

"If we don't want to enter into a ministry partnership with someone who spends all their time begging for money on the Internet, what's our other option?" Michelle asked.

"There are plenty of websites that offer ministry opportunities," Matthew said. "The only problem is they charge several hundred dollars per day, which can add up to a lot of money if we wanted to volunteer our time for several weeks. Many of these websites spend thousands of dollars on advertising to get on top of the search results. They even offer people looking for ministry opportunities a search finder function, so all you need to do is enter the keyword *Africa,* and it will bring up hundreds of results."

"My mom's friend had a terrible experience with one of those organizations," Michelle said. "She received an email invitation looking for volunteers to help the orphaned children in Ukraine. She had to pay for her own flight and was promised room and board at the orphanage, but the ministry environment was terrible.

"The company who set up the trip fulfilled all of their obligations by providing transportation to and from the airport, along with a private room and hot meals, but the women who worked at the orphanage didn't want or need any help. They treated my mom's friend like she had the plague. They looked at her with suspicion and contempt, wondering why an American would travel all the way to Ukraine to interact with their children."

"I found a similar ministry opportunity for construction work in Honduras," Matthew said. "They were charging two hundred dollars per day for people who wanted to volunteer their time mixing cement by hand and painting buildings. The price included food, lodging, ground transportation, emergency medical insurance and a free T-shirt."

"We could offer an even better deal at the Rescue Mission," Michelle said.

"What do you mean?" Matthew asked.

"If we charged two hundred dollars per day for volunteers who wanted to work with the homeless, we could pick them up at the airport and put them up in a hotel room for fifty dollars per night," Michelle said. "That way we could make over a hundred dollars per person. If we had a group of ten volunteers, we could be making over a thousand dollars per day."

"Why not keep all the money for ourselves and let the volunteers sleep on the floor with the homeless?" Matthew said. "The volunteers could also eat three free meals per day at the Rescue Mission and it wouldn't cost us anything, except for the commission we would have to pay the Internet advertising company."

"If we don't want to enter into a ministry

partnership with a company that advertises on the Internet in an attempt to find volunteers who are willing to pay two hundred dollars per day for low-quality ministry opportunities, what would be our third option?" Michelle asked.

"I think we should book a one-way flight to Nairobi," Matthew said. "Then after we rent several low-priced hotel rooms near a nice supermarket, we could start visiting churches in the area and meeting with local pastors. After meeting the pastors and listening to them preach, we will know which ones can be trusted and which ones to avoid. Once we find several good pastors that can be trusted, I'm sure they will know of other evangelists or missionaries in the area that could help us accomplish anything we wanted to do in Kenya."

"I will also start asking around at my church to see if anyone has any ministry connections in Kenya," Michelle said as she gave her fiancé a kiss good night.

* * *

During the next several months, Matthew continued preaching three messages per week at the Rescue Mission while Michelle worked part-time as the events coordinator for Christian Singles International. When the day of the art gallery fundraising event arrived, Monica arranged the upper and lower levels with over two hundred homeless signs, while Matthew and Michelle set up several tables with refreshments and a portable microphone system.

When the upper and lower levels were filled with guests, Monica lowered the volume of the classical music that was playing on the overhead speakers. Shortly after, Matthew turned on the portable sound equipment, picked up the microphone, and said to the audience, "Tonight is a special occasion for celebration. I know many people here this evening have been praying for a homeless woman named Amber Rose Thunderhawk.

"Several months ago, Amber was sleeping on a piece of cardboard underneath an outdoor billboard sign when she was attacked at night. The perpetrator tried to kill her using a cinder block. The men who found her rolled up in a bloody blanket the following morning said they could see her brain exposed through a large gash in her skull.

"Nobody thought Amber would live, but by God's grace and the power of your prayers, she has made a remarkable recovery. After she was released from the hospital, social services got involved and provided her with a caseworker and her very own apartment. Her new home only has one room with a tiny bathroom, but it came fully furnished with everything she needed to be self-sufficient. When I stopped by to see her last week, she was clean and sober and so very happy."

Because many people in the audience started clapping and expressing their gratitude, Matthew paused his message momentarily, then continued by saying, "I wanted to share Amber's healing journey with you this evening, along with a collection of homeless signs, in an attempt to raise awareness. Although many of these signs are creative expressions of art, they have also been used on the streets to raise money. Many of the homeless men and women who created these signs earn between twenty and thirty dollars per day. When a woman uses one of these signs, she is able to earn around fifty dollars per day. During Christmas, when everybody is feeling more generous, a woman can earn up to eighty dollars per day.

"Many of the homeless men and women who created these signs are drug addicts and alcoholics. I know several men who will drink a half-gallon of vodka per day. They will hold up their sign on a busy intersection for most of the day, and once they acquire enough money to buy a bottle, they will run to the nearest liquor store and spend the rest of the evening getting drunk. On other days, two or three homeless men will pool their resources together to rent a hotel room for the night. After they take a shower and get cleaned up, they will start the process all over again the next day.

"As difficult as it is for many of the homeless men and women who are living on the streets of America to exist, there are people in the world today who have it so much worse. In many large cities in America, it's possible to get free meals three times per day. Because America is one of the wealthiest nations in the world, we can offer our homeless population free food, free overnight shelter, free showers and free restroom facilities. We also have free detoxification centers, free traveler's aid, free bus tokens and free employment resources.

"In some of the poorest countries of the world, it's not possible to get a free meal because most of the citizens of that country would be standing in line. Let me give you some examples from the World Bank that demonstrate just how bad it is for the homeless population in many third-world countries.

"The World Bank has a method to determine the poorest countries in the world by dividing the number of income-producing citizens by their earnings and wages. These figures are calculated in the country's local currency and then converted into American dollars at the current exchange rate. For example, the average household income in America is around seventy thousand dollars per year. At the bottom of the list, there are countries in Africa where the average citizen earns less than one dollar per day.

"Burundi is one of the poorest countries in the world because the average citizen only earns seventy cents per day. Mozambique is a little better at one dollar and thirty-five cents per day. In Haiti, the average citizen earns five dollars per day, and in Kenya, the average citizen earns five dollars and seventy cents per day.[2]

"When you see a young woman from Kenya sitting on the sidewalk, holding a small child and begging for money, you know the situation is desperate. If the average citizen in Kenya earns less than five dollars per day, it's very unlikely that the woman will be able to receive enough money to feed herself and her child.

"Although the Kenyan government will not officially say that their citizens are starving to death, what will happen is that the woman's health will continue to deteriorate to the point where her life expectancy will be greatly reduced. Because the young woman will not be able to eat enough healthy foods, even though she didn't technically starve to death, she will eventually die of health-related complications that were caused by malnutrition.

"Even though the homeless situation in Kenya is very desperate, it gives American missionaries a great advantage for several reasons. First of all, it only costs sixty dollars to buy a hundred-pound bag of rice in Kenya, which will feed a lot of elderly women and young children. If the average citizen in Kenya only earns five dollars per day, it would be possible to hire several local evangelists to help spread the Gospel message. If you paid three local evangelists ten dollars per day, and if they worked three days per week setting up outreach locations, you could produce a lot of heavenly treasure for a very small amount of money.

"Because American missionaries have a great opportunity to produce a rich harvest for the kingdom of heaven in third-world countries, Michelle and I would like to ask for your support. We would like to spend the next several months in Kenya conducting outreaches in some of the world's largest slums. We want to proclaim the Gospel message to those who have never heard the truth about Jesus."

After Matthew finished speaking, there was an awkward moment of silence throughout the entire gallery until one man said, "I would like to make a donation."

"Your donations to African Missionaries are one hundred percent tax deductible," Matthew said. "You can make a donation online through our website or by sending us a check."

"We will also be accepting cash and credit card donations at the front counter," Michelle said. "Anything you can do to help us would be greatly appreciated."

After Monica restored the classical music to the overhead speakers, the art gallery erupted with the joyful sound of private conversations. Soon after, Daniel approached Matthew and Michelle with Rebecca at his side and said, "We wanted to make the first donation. I know it's not much, but here's a check for two thousand dollars, along with two tickets to Nairobi."

"Thank you so much!" Michelle said as she gave each of them a hug.

"The tickets are only one-way, but they are fully refundable," Daniel said. "I know you wanted to travel around August third, but they didn't have any available flights, so I booked you a few days sooner, on the last day of July."

"That will work out perfectly," Matthew said. "You have been a faithful and true friend ever since the day we met. I can't thank you enough."

* * *

When Draven discovered the missionaries' travel

plans, he reported back to Narco-Leóna and said, "The monkeys were able to raise a large sum of money. They are planning to leave our territory and travel to Africa."

"I want you to follow them wherever they go," Narco-Leóna said. "Once you discover their final destination, work with the local leadership to bring about their destruction."

"I won't stop until they're dead," Draven said.

* * *

At the end of the evening, after the missionaries had finished thanking all their guests for their generous financial contributions, Monica added up the proceeds and said, "We brought in a little over ten thousand dollars. Two thousand of that came from Daniel and Rebecca, so you don't owe me a commission on that amount."

"It sounds like we owe you eight hundred dollars," Michelle said.

"I also wanted to make a financial contribution to your work in Kenya," Monica said. "How about you pay me five hundred dollars to rent the art gallery for the evening and help me set up the next exhibit early tomorrow morning?"

"Thank you so much," Michelle said. "We would love to help you tomorrow morning."

* * *

The following day, after the missionaries finished helping Monica set up an elaborate modern art display, Matthew submitted a thirty-day notice to his landlord and rented a storage unit near Mrs. Nobility's house. He also called the Rescue Mission to cut back on his chapel service provider schedule. When Chaplain Hemingway answered the phone, he said, "We are going to miss you so much. You have an authentic gift at preaching. You are the best street preacher that I have ever met."

"You're too kind," Matthew said. "It's only going to be a few months. Michelle and I will be back before you know it."

"I know a lot of our guests are going to miss you as well," the Chaplain said. "You have changed the lives of many for the better, and we will be forever grateful for your service."

"Thank you for your kind words of support," Matthew said. "I will keep in touch and send you plenty of updates from the mission field."

2nd CHAPTER

Missionaries

After the missionaries made all the final arrangements, they spent several weeks saying goodbye to all their friends. Before loading the essentials into their backpacks, they asked Michelle's mother for a ride to the airport.

"Of course, I will drive you to the airport," Mrs. Nobility said. "I'm so proud of you both. It brings me so much joy to see my daughter giving up everything to serve the Lord in the mission field. I'm also very concerned for your safety. You have to promise me you will not do anything that's dangerous."

"I will watch over Michelle with my very life," Matthew said. "Nothing bad is going to happen to us. We will not do anything stupid or dangerous."

"I love you so much," Mrs. Nobility said as she started crying.

"Mom, please don't cry," Michelle said as she leaned forward to give her mother a hug. "The Lord will watch over us. I have so much peace in my heart. I know everything is going to be okay."

When Mrs. Nobility dropped the missionaries off at the airport, she said, "I will be praying for an outpouring of the Holy Spirit's power to flow through your ministry efforts every day."

"Thank you for your prayer support," Michelle said. "You know it means a lot to me. I promise to send you updates every chance I get. I will send the first report as soon as we arrive in Nairobi."

"I love you both very much," Mrs. Nobility said, giving them one last hug and kiss goodbye.

* * *

Several hours later, when the missionaries were in transit to the London Heathrow Airport, Matthew leaned over and said, "I would like to add a few more items to our list of rules."

"What kind of items?" Michelle asked. "We have so many rules, I can barely keep track of them."

"Then let's start from the beginning," Matthew said. "The first rule existed before we were engaged, and that is no sex until marriage. I would like to add a subcategory to that rule—no intimate activities that will lead to sex before marriage."

"I agree with rule number one," Michelle said. "My Bible says we need to keep the marriage bed pure and undefiled because God will judge fornicators and adulterers."[3]

"You are the one who made rule number two, which is we will not invite homeless people, drug addicts or alcoholics into our homes to live with us," Matthew said. "I also added a subcategory to that rule, that we will not bring wild animals into our homes either. I probably need to add a subcategory to the rule about wild animals, because in Africa, they don't give their pets rabies shots.

"I realize it may be very tempting to feed a group of monkeys on the side of the road, but it can be very dangerous. The monkeys can start fighting amongst themselves and even jump on you and start climbing up your leg to get the last piece of banana. If you get bitten or scratched by a monkey, dog or bat with rabies, you will need emergency medical treatment within the first twenty-four hours. Once the rabies virus enters into your nervous system, the disease is always fatal for humans."

"I agree with that rule," Michelle said. "I will not feed the monkeys on the side of the road, or pet any wild animals in Africa."

"The third rule is that we don't get separated on international mission trips or when we are ministering in dangerous neighborhoods," Matthew said. "A subcategory to that rule would concern the use of motorcycle taxis. If we're working in a rural countryside village, it would probably be safe to take two motorbikes to get to our destination; but if we are in Nairobi ministering in a dangerous neighborhood, and there are criminal gangs that are constantly looking around to kidnap American tourists, then we probably need to ride on the same bike."

"Can you fit three people on a motorcycle taxi?" Michelle asked.

"I think so," Matthew said. "I promised your mom nothing bad would happen to us, so it's important that we stay together."

"What's the fourth rule?" Michelle asked.

"I only want us to eat food that we have prepared ourselves," Matthew said. "I don't want either one of us getting sick, and this rule is so serious that I'm even concerned about eating the airplane food on our next flight."

"What's wrong with our next flight?" Michelle asked.

"I'm sure the flight will be fine," Matthew said. "My concern is the bacteria that's present in foreign countries. In America, we have bacteria all over the place, but it doesn't bother us or make us sick because we are used to eating it. The United Kingdom and Egypt have different strains of bacteria, so it's possible the airplane food could give us a bad case of Delhi belly, Montezuma's revenge or even the Aztec two-step.

"To apply rule number four, let's stop viewing our food from the perspective of whether or not it tastes good, but from the perspective of a potential bacteria risk. For example, let's not eat the airplane salad because I'm sure somebody washed the lettuce in tap water, and it's probably covered with bacteria. If we order the pasta main course, and it's steaming hot and covered in foil, then it's probably safe to eat because the heat will kill the bacteria. If our dinner rolls come sealed in plastic, they are safe to eat. If the dinner rolls have been left out in the open air, and the airline stewardess who has been in contact with all the other passengers handles our dinner rolls with her plastic gloves that have been exposed to all the germs on this airplane, then let's not eat the dinner rolls."

"Rule number four is no dinner rolls," Michelle said.

"This is very serious," Matthew said. "There are open sewers all over the place in Africa. All it would take to make us very sick is one fly that has been crawling around in the open sewers. If that fly entered the kitchen window of a restaurant and crawled all over our food, we could get typhoid, and it's very painful. Although we have already had our oral typhoid medication, I don't want us eating or drinking anything that we haven't prepared ourselves."

"What if a pastor invites us to his house for dinner?" Michelle asked.

"We have to be very careful on how we handle those kinds of situations," Matthew said. "One option is to explain our concerns to the pastor, and if he is filled with the Holy Spirit, and if the Holy Spirit knows about rule number four, then the pastor will not press his hospitality on us. Another option for dealing with a pastor who wants to share a meal with us would be to invite him back to our apartment for dinner."

"We could also get some store-bought dinner rolls

that have been sealed in a plastic container and share those with the man," Michelle said.

"Rule number four is important because there's a good chance the pastor will not have any refrigeration," Matthew said. "If he wants to serve us meat, it's probably some kind of bush meat that we shouldn't be eating anyway. Or maybe his neighbor slaughtered a goat last week and it has been covered with flies ever since.

"Rule number four also applies to our beverages. I'm sure there will be a time when a pastor's wife will invite us into her home and serve us hot tea. Even though the heat from the boiling water will kill all the bacteria, our host will want to serve us the tea in a cup that she washed with river water.

"Even though the river water will not make our host sick, it will make us very sick, because a few hundred yards up the stream, there's probably a herd of cattle that have been defecating in the water supply. So rule number four is very simple, we don't put anything in our mouths that we didn't prepare ourselves in a clean and sterile environment."

"I agree with rule number four," Michelle said. "I'm sorry for giving you a hard time earlier."

"I'm also concerned about our bottled water," Matthew said. "Even if we buy the best name-brand bottled water, it's still going to contain bacteria and other microscopic particles that we are not used to drinking, so that's why I brought along some food-grade hydrogen peroxide.

"All we need to do is mix a small capful of food-grade hydrogen peroxide into a five-gallon container of purified drinking water. After waiting several hours, it should be safe to drink. If the water still makes us feel a little queasy the following day, we can add another capful to see if that helps."

"What's the difference between food-grade hydrogen peroxide and other grades?" Michelle asked.

"Food-grade is safe for food production because it doesn't contain any of the harmful chemicals that are present in the medical-grade," Matthew said.

"Are there any more rules that I need to know about?" Michelle asked.

"We need to protect ourselves from malaria and other diseases that are transmitted by mosquitoes," Matthew said. "When a mosquito lands on your skin, the first thing it does is inject your body with an anti-blood-clotting fluid, which causes a red, itchy bump to appear a few days later. If the mosquito is carrying malaria parasites, those parasites will enter your body when the anti-blood-clotting fluid is injected.

"Once malaria parasites enter your bloodstream, they will travel around your body until they reach your liver. After they enter a person's liver, they will start laying eggs. When those eggs hatch, that's when a person gets very sick with malaria. It's a very painful and deadly disease, and I don't want either one of us to get sick with malaria."

"I thought the nurse at the travel clinic gave us a

prescription for an anti-malarial drug that will prevent us from getting sick," Michelle said.

"It's called Atovaquone-Proguanil," Matthew said. "This drug is used to prevent and treat malaria, but we don't have enough for an extended period of time."

"Why didn't we buy enough when we were still in America?" Michelle asked.

"Because the drug is very expensive, and you know how I don't like putting anything unnatural in my body," Matthew said. "We have enough to treat both of us if we get sick with malaria, and we also have several weeks' worth of supplies as a preventative measure, but we don't have enough if you want to take one tablet every day for the next several months."

"How do we protect ourselves?" Michelle asked.

"Because it's possible to get malaria even when taking anti-malarial medications every day, and because most people who live in Africa don't take anti-malarial drugs on a daily basis, the best way to protect ourselves is by not getting stung by mosquitoes in the first place," Matthew said. "Which brings us to rule number five: We cannot have any exposed skin, except for our hands and faces. This rule also applies to us even when we are inside our own apartments at night."

"Rule five is no exposed skin?" Michelle asked.

"If we are going to deliver the Gospel message to Muslims, you should already be familiar with that rule," Matthew said. "I'm not asking you to wear a burka, which would also be a very effective way of keeping mosquitoes away from your face; but we need to protect ourselves from getting stung, and the best way to do that is by wearing long-sleeve safari shirts and full-length pants with socks."

"I understand why this rule would be important if we are going to be working with Muslims, but why is it important that we keep covered up at night, even when we are inside our own apartments?" Michelle asked.

"That's because one type of mosquito comes out at night and another type of mosquito will try to sting us in the early morning hours," Matthew said. "Depending on the construction of our hotel rooms, there may not be any screens on the windows, and there's probably going to be huge gaps underneath the doors.

"Even if the windows will close all the way, they probably won't close tight enough to keep mosquitoes out. That's why it's important that we have mosquito nets over our beds at night, or else we need to sleep in our mosquito-proof camping tents."

"Let me see if I understand what you are saying," Michelle said. "We don't have enough anti-malarial medication for an extended period of time; so our plan to protect ourselves is to avoid getting stung by mosquitoes in the first place. We can accomplish this by wearing long-sleeve shirts and full-length pants with socks, and by sleeping underneath our mosquito nets at night."

"Exactly," Matthew said.

"Have you considered using mosquito repellent?" Michelle asked.

"Anything that we can do to protect ourselves would be great," Matthew said. "If we can find some natural mosquito repellent that doesn't have any harmful chemicals, that would be even better."

"What about wearing a beekeeper's outfit during the day?" Michelle asked.

"I realize this is a difficult rule with many complex parts, but let me summarize it for you so that we can agree upon the best way to protect ourselves from getting sick," Matthew said. "I think we should take our first dose of anti-malarial medication on the plane and another tablet when we arrive in Nairobi. That way, we will have some of the drug in our system in case we get stung by mosquitoes on our way to the hotel.

"Once we check into our hotel rooms, I will inspect the windows and doors to mosquito-proof any openings. If the windows don't have any screens, and there are big gaps between the metal frames, we could tape them shut and place a blanket in front of our doors at night. We will also need to make sure our mosquito nets are tucked underneath the mattress all the way around the bed so that there are no openings. If we use mosquito repellent and wear full-length clothing that doesn't allow for any exposed skin, then we should be okay.

"If we don't hear any mosquitoes buzzing around our beds at night, and if we don't see any mosquitoes in our rooms during the day, then there's no need to take the anti-malarial medication on a regular basis. If we find ourselves ministering in the middle of a swamp, and if there are millions of mosquitoes all around us, then we should be taking several different types of anti-malarial medication on a daily basis and wearing our beekeeping outfits at all times."

"I agree with rule number five," Michelle said. "Once we get settled in Nairobi, I will look around for some lemon eucalyptus oils or a lavender herbal extract that we can use as a natural mosquito repellent."

"There's one more security issue that we should talk about before we arrive," Matthew said. "In America, we have rights as American citizens, but in Kenya, we don't have any rights because we are entering the country on a tourist visa. We will need to obey all the Kenyan laws, even if we don't know what those laws are. We will also need to be very careful when dealing with the police."

"What's wrong with the police?" Michelle asked.

"We are starting to see more news stories about how the police in America have been abusing their powers, but it's even worse in third-world countries," Matthew said. "I have heard stories from missionaries working in Nigeria about how a police officer pulled his gun and pointed it in a man's face. Once the police officer had the man's complete attention, he said, 'What did you bring to Nigeria to give to me?'"

"What would be the best way to deal with that situation?" Michelle asked.

"It would be important to remain calm and friendly," Matthew said. "I would probably start the conversation by complimenting the officer on his uniform. I would tell him how professional he looks wearing the uniform because it makes him look strong and dignified. Then I would transition the conversation over to how much I like his country and offer to take him to a restaurant and buy him some tea. If the officer wasn't in the mood to visit a restaurant, then I would offer to give him some tea money."

"What's tea money?" Michelle asked.

"In Kenya, they refer to *tea money* as a friendly way of paying a person a bribe," Matthew said. "If we were best friends with the police officer, we would take him to a restaurant and cover the cost of the biscuits and tea. If the officer wasn't in the mood to visit the restaurant, then we would find a friendly way of giving him some cash.

"That's why it's important to have a few dollars in our front pockets in case of an emergency. It's also important to keep your tea money separate from your passport, credit cards and the rest of your cash. You don't want to pull out a thick wallet stuffed full of cash and give the officer a few dollars because he will not be satisfied. If you show a corrupt police officer a lot of cash, he will find a way of motivating you to give it all away. So that's why it's important to keep your tea money separate and in a place that's easy to access."

"Maybe we should hide our money in several locations, so that if one area is compromised, at least we will have backup funds in another location," Michelle said.

"It's also going to be important to watch out for

pickpockets," Matthew said. "That's why I like wearing these military-style pants. My travel wallet fits perfectly inside my side pocket. I would instantly know if some-one were trying to get inside my pocket, because it's secured by two large buttons that are impossible to open without a lot of pulling and tugging."

"I was planning on keeping my purse inside my daypack," Michelle said. "There's a small compartment inside the main storage area that zips shut, and my purse fits perfectly inside."

"Once we set foot outside the international airport, we are going to become a target," Matthew said. "In Nigeria, there are criminal gangs who are constantly watching the airport at night in an attempt to find American citizens to kidnap. Although Kenya is a lot safer than South Africa, Somalia and Nigeria, we still need to be very careful."

* * *

After several layovers on three different continents, the missionaries finally arrived at Nairobi's Jomo Kenyatta International Airport. It was ten o'clock at night, and they needed to purchase a six-month visa and pass through customs and immigration before picking up their backpacks from the luggage area.

When they walked outside, they could smell the scent of burning wood in the air. After looking up in wonder at the star-filled night sky, they began walking around and noticed a man holding a sign that displayed the names "Matthew & Michelle Goodwin."

"You must be Charles," Matthew said as he approached the man.

"Welcome to Kenya," Charles said. "My car is right over here."

After Charles helped the missionaries load their backpacks into the trunk of his car, he paid the airport parking fee and began the forty-minute journey to the retreat center.

"I didn't realize Nairobi was so big," Michelle said.

"There are over five million people who live in the city and the surrounding suburbs," Charles said. "Are you planning to visit any of our world-class safari destinations?"

"We are here for a mission trip," Michelle said, "although I would like to go on a safari to see how the wild animals interact in their natural habitats."

"I would be happy to drive you around and show you all the sights," Charles said. "Why did you choose the Sacred Heart Retreat Center for your lodging?"

"The price was higher than many of the hotels in the area," Matthew said, "but from the description and images on the Internet, it looked like a nice place."

"Very nice, indeed," Charles said. "There are twenty-two religious sisters who operate the retreat center. We have eighty-five self-contained boarding rooms and a large conference hall with a cafeteria and a chapel. It's a popular venue for Catholic retreats, conferences and weddings."

"It sounds very nice," Michelle said.

"We also have full-time security guards, plenty of guest parking and laundry services," Charles said. "The chapel is open twenty-four hours per day, so you are welcome to join the sisters for morning and evening prayer. I will give you my cell number in case you need a ride anywhere in the city."

"Thank you," Matthew said. "I was originally attracted to this location because it's close to one of the world's largest slums. According to a map on the Internet, there should also be a shopping mall and a grocery store a few blocks away."

"At the Koto-Bobby Junction, you will find one of Nairobi's finest supermarkets," Charles said. "It's surrounded by many smaller shops, and there's even a money exchange service."

"It sounds like we will have everything we need," Michelle said as Charles sounded the car horn, and the security guard opened the gate to the retreat center.

3rd CHAPTER

The following morning, the missionaries walked over to the grocery store to buy supplies. After acquiring all the groceries they needed for several days, Matthew purchased an electric hotplate that used two hundred and twenty volt electricity. He wanted to hard-boil some eggs for breakfast, while Michelle prepared a fruit salad that consisted of papayas, mangos and bananas.

After they spent a day getting adjusted to their new environment, Matthew called Pastor Emeka and said, "We arrived last night and would like to meet you tomorrow morning. Can you meet us at the Koto-Bobby Junction? There's a restaurant on the northeast corner where we can discuss future ministry plans."

"It's going to be very difficult for me to travel to your location," Pastor Emeka said. "How about you come to Ngomongo Village so that we can discuss your plans at my church?"

"We have only been here one day," Matthew said. "We don't know how to use public transportation, and I don't know where Ngomongo Village is or how to find your church. It would be better for you to come to the Koto-Bobby Junction because everybody seems to know where that's located."

"I will call you around ten o'clock in the morning when I reach the junction," Pastor Emeka said.

When Pastor Emeka arrived for the meeting, the missionaries greeted him at the restaurant. After being seated at a table near the back, Michelle started the conversation by saying, "Matthew told me you met over the Internet and that you have a desire to help the orphans and widows."

"That's true," Pastor Emeka said.

"He needed financial support, so I sent him one hundred dollars," Matthew said. "After spending the money on food, Pastor Emeka sent me pictures of little kids eating a pile of rice that was being served on a large banana leaf."

"There are many orphaned children in my area who come to my church," Pastor Emeka said. "One or both of their parents have died, and they are living with their closest relatives. Because no one can afford to send these children to school, they have nothing to do all day, so they come to my church looking for food."

"That sounds awfully sad," Michelle said. "What can we do to help?"

"It costs a lot of money to support these children," Pastor Emeka said.

"When Michelle and I were praying about this trip,

I felt called to deliver the Gospel message to Muslims," Matthew said. "Do you know of any opportunities where we can minister to Muslims?"

"Why would you want to do that?" Pastor Emeka asked. "The Muslims are very difficult here. They don't interact very well with Christians. If you are an authentic Christian, you should be helping your brothers and sisters in Christ."

"We would be more than happy to help the Christians in your area, although I'm still feeling called to minister to the Muslims," Matthew said. "As you know, God desires that all men hear the Gospel message and repent of their sins. In addition to fulfilling the Great Commission by proclaiming the Gospel message to those who have never heard the truth about Jesus Christ, we need to evaluate our ministry activities very carefully to make sure we are using our limited resources very wisely."

"We have very serious ministry needs," Pastor Emeka said. "I know people who are so poor they are eating leaves off the trees."

"Because it costs a lot of time and money to travel to Africa, we want to use our resources wisely," Matthew said. "I just don't think the best use of our time and re-sources would be spent on ministering to the Christians in your church. As a pastor, it is your job to minister to them, and as an evangelist, it's my job to proclaim the Gospel message to non-believers."

"It will never work," Pastor Emeka said. "The

Muslims in Kenya are way too difficult. Many Christian missionaries have tried sharing their faith, and it always turns violent."

"There are two different ministry approaches when it comes to dealing with Muslims," Matthew said. "One approach would be to acknowledge any elements of 'goodness and truth' found in their religion as a preliminary preparation for the Gospel message.[4] The other approach would be to challenge them to be better Muslims by accepting the truth about the Messiah that's contained in the Quran."

"Are you a Christian or a Muslim?" Pastor Emeka asked. "As Christians, we need to preach from the Bible. The god of Islam is not the same as the God of Christianity."

"Let's take a look at what the Bible says about being an evangelist for Christ," Matthew said. "I would like to use an example from the life of Saint Paul. In the First Letter to the Corinthians, in the ninth chapter, Saint Paul says that although I am free to all, I have made myself a slave to all, so that I may win more souls to Christ."[5]

"Let me look up that passage," Pastor Emeka said as he removed a black, hard-covered Bible from his bag.

"In verse twenty, Saint Paul says, 'To the Jews I became as a Jew, in order to win Jews.'[6] To those outside the law I became as one outside the law so that I might win those outside the law. 'To the weak I became weak, so that I might win the weak. I have become all things to all people, that I might by all means save some.'[7]

"Now let's look at how we can apply that Scripture passage to our own lives," Matthew said. "I'm sure if Saint Paul were alive today, he would become more like the Muslims in order to win the Muslims to Christ. If you want to follow Saint Paul's example of ministry that's clearly defined in Sacred Scripture, you would need to become more like the Muslims in order to win the Muslims to Christ."

"We experienced the power of that Scripture passage when we started working with the homeless," Michelle said. "I remember how uncomfortable I felt wearing the latest fashions on skid row when everybody else was dressed in several layers of old clothing that hadn't been washed all week. When I became more like the homeless, I was able to connect with them better, and the better I was able to connect with the homeless, the more fruit our ministry efforts produced."

"It's never going to work," Pastor Emeka said. "The Muslims in Kenya are way too radicalized."

"I would like to preach to the Muslims using the Quran because it's their own holy book," Matthew said. "If a Muslim evangelist came into an Islamic community with several bags of rice, and wanted to share a spiritual message from the Quran in an attempt to help them become better Muslims by accepting the truth about the Messiah, then I'm sure they would welcome him with open arms and there wouldn't be any problems."

"Christians only preach from the Bible," Pastor Emeka said. "By preaching from the Quran, you would be setting a bad example for the youth. It would cause too much confusion. It will never work."

"I can show you several examples from the Bible where Saint Paul used references from pagan sources when he was preaching to non-believers," Matthew said. "He did this in an attempt to build bridges between the truth of the Gospel and his non-believing audience."

"Where's that located in the Bible?" Pastor Emeka asked.

"When Saint Paul was ministering in Athens, he noticed a pagan altar with the inscription, 'To an unknown god.'[8] He used this example to start his message by saying, 'What therefore you worship as unknown,' I would like to proclaim to you.[9] He then continued his message by quoting a Greek poet by saying, 'As even some of your own poets have said, "For we too are his offspring."'[10] The pagan source that Paul is quoting to a non-believing audience has become part of God's Word."

"Where is that located in the Bible?" Pastor Emeka asked.

"It's in the seventeenth chapter of Acts," Matthew said. "In Saint Paul's letter to Titus, he quotes another secular source by saying, 'It was one of them, their very own prophet, who said, "Cretans are always liars, vicious brutes, lazy gluttons."'[11] Then in the First Letter to the Corinthians, Saint Paul quotes a Greek proverb that has also become a part of Sacred Scripture by saying, 'Let us eat and drink, for tomorrow we die.'[12]

"As you can see, Saint Paul used many different references from pagan sources to make a point to a non-Jewish audience. He is not quoting these sources as a way to validate what the pagans are saying; rather, he is using them to build bridges with his audience so that he can deliver the Gospel message."

"I can't find that verse," Pastor Emeka said.

"If you want to be an effective evangelist for Christ, it's important to follow Saint Paul's example that's clearly defined in Sacred Scripture," Matthew said. "When Saint Paul was preaching to a Jewish audience, he used passages of Scripture from the Torah and the Old Testament prophets. When Saint Paul was proclaiming the Gospel message to a Gentile audience, he used quotes from the Greek proverbs and poets. If Saint Paul were alive today, he would use passages from the Quran when proclaiming the Gospel message to Muslims.

"The reason why I like quoting passages from the Quran when preaching to Muslims is because the Quran confirms the authority of the Scriptures. For example, the word *scripture* is used over two hundred times in the Quran, and the phrase *People of the Book* or *People of the Scripture* is used over thirty times. The Quran also says that the Psalms are divinely inspired and speaks about them in five different surahs."[13]

"How about you give me twenty thousand shillings and I will set up an outreach for you next week," Pastor Emeka said. "We will gather all the non-believers together under a shade canopy so you can proclaim the Gospel message of our Lord and Savior Jesus Christ."

"That sounds like a lot of money," Michelle said. "How much is twenty thousand shillings in American dollars?"

"It's about two hundred dollars," Matthew said.

"I have a man on ground who can set everything up," Pastor Emeka said. "He has been working in the area as an evangelist for many years. It's about a two-hour drive on the outskirts of Nairobi."

"Maybe we should pray about it and seek the Lord's guidance," Michelle said.

"I'm asking on behalf of the children," Pastor Emeka said. "You promised to help the orphans and widows in my area. I need money to travel back home. I had to travel many hours to meet with you today. Please give me ten thousand shillings so that I can travel back to my house, and an additional twenty thousand shillings to set up the outreach."

"How about we give you five thousand shillings today, five thousand shillings when we visit your church on Sunday, and ten thousand shillings after you set up a successful outreach location?" Matthew asked.

"Please give me thirty thousand shillings today, and I will set up the most excellent outreach location for you," Pastor Emeka said.

"We just arrived in Nairobi and need more time to find a better money exchange service," Michelle said.

"How about six thousand shillings right now so

that you can travel back home?" Matthew said. "When we visit your church on Sunday, we will bring you more money."

"Very well," Pastor Emeka said as he picked up the shillings that Matthew had placed on the table.

* * *

When Draven discovered the missionaries' plans, he softened his shadow-stalking appearance and made his presence known to the demonic spirits who were guarding one of Dragon-Claw's government buildings. "I'm here on assignment," Draven said.

"What do you want?" the security officer asked.

"I seek Dragon-Claw's permission to operate in his territory," Draven said.

"Let him pass by," the security officer said.

When Draven entered into Dragon-Claw's presence, he said, "I have been assigned to destroy two American missionaries who are operating in your area. I only ask for your cooperation. Once they are eliminated, I will return to my own territory."

"What makes you think we need your help?" Dragon-Claw asked.

"I am only following orders," Draven said, bowing down in submission.

"Missionaries from America don't last more than a few weeks when they come here," Dragon-Claw said. "The food they eat will make them so sick it will be excreted from their filthy bodies before they know what hit them. It's even better when they visit one of our hospitals because we will infect them with recycled needles, along with an onslaught of airborne pathogens that will send them packing faster than those monkeys can say, 'Emergency medical flight back home.'"

"I'm only asking your permission to follow them around and work with your commanders to bring about their destruction," Draven said.

"You have my permission," Dragon-Claw said.

* * *

After the missionaries paid for Pastor Emeka's meal, they walked outside the restaurant and watched him jump on the back of a motorcycle taxi.

"There's no way it costs one hundred dollars for public transportation to travel around Nairobi," Matthew said. "I'm sure the locals know how to get around for a few dollars per day."

"I'm sure we are going to learn a lot more about Pastor Emeka when we visit his church on Sunday," Michelle said.

"Maybe the Lord will open up better ministry opportunities for us through his man-on-ground," Matthew said. "In the meantime, let's visit some local churches to see if we can find a few Godly men who have a heart to serve the Lord in the mission field."

* * *

When Sunday morning arrived, the driver that Pastor Emeka hired picked up the missionaries at the retreat center. Because his gas tank was almost empty, he pulled into the nearest gas station and said, "Pastor

Emeka said that you would provide petrol for the journey. I used all my money to drive here because it's a very great distance."

After the man filled the tank on his four-door Toyota Corolla, he said to Matthew, "The station attendant needs to be paid 6,890 shillings."

"That's about seventy dollars," Matthew said, handing over the money.

The first part of the journey seemed to pass very quickly as the driver navigated through the center of Nairobi using a series of two-lane highways and thoroughfares. The second part of the journey was more difficult when the paved highways turned into dusty roads with deep crevasses and treacherous potholes. After about an hour and forty minutes had passed, the missionaries reached Pastor Emeka's home, which was surrounded by jacaranda trees with purple blossoms.

The church, located next to Pastor Emeka's house, was about twelve by twenty feet with cinder block walls and a dirt floor. The tin roof that covered the structure had been painted white many years ago, but since that time, most of the paint had faded away.

When the missionaries stepped out of the vehicle, Pastor Emeka and his wife gave them a warm welcome. After a brief introduction, they were escorted to the front of the church and offered a place of honor sitting next to the elders who were facing the audience.

"We have invited the entire community," Pastor Emeka said.

Because only a few people were seated in the audience on wooden benches, Matthew asked, "How many people are you expecting today?"

"They are coming," Pastor Emeka said. "As soon as the music begins, they will arrive."

Fifteen minutes later, three musicians and several teenage girls took their places in the front of the church and started worshiping the Lord with a festive style of African dance. Not long after, the church slowly began to fill with about fifty members.

When it came time for Pastor Emeka to introduce his guests, he invited the missionaries to stand next to him as the audience welcomed them with a warm round of applause. After taking up a collection, Pastor Emeka proceeded to preach a message by screaming into the microphone using a different preaching voice than he would normally use during his regular conversations.

Halfway through the message, Michelle leaned over and whispered in Matthew's ear, "Can you understand what he is saying?"

"I think he's preaching in English, but with that heavy African accent and all the popping and hissing noise from the microphone, I don't think anyone can understand what he is saying," Matthew said.

After the service ended, the missionaries were quickly escorted out of the church and into Pastor Emeka's home, where they were offered a seat on the couch. A few minutes later, the church elders arrived and sat down next to them. When Pastor Emeka entered the room, his wife brought out a pitcher of water and a rinsing bowl and began pouring water on everybody's hands so they could wash them before the meal.

Just before the food was served, Matthew said, "I hope you will be able to excuse us from sharing a meal with you today."

"Why won't you share a meal with us?" Pastor Emeka asked. "My wife cooked a community dinner for all our members because you promised to support the orphans and widows in my church."

"It's not that we don't want to share a meal with you," Matthew said. "We're on a special diet and have to be very careful that we don't get sick."

"We did bring some appetizers that we would like to share with you," Michelle said as she opened her daypack and took out several packages of gingersnap cookies. "We purchased a large box of these to share with your congregation."

After Pastor Emeka's wife served the meal and everybody started eating, Matthew stood up and said, "Will you please excuse me? I would like to walk around outside and pray while you are eating."

"I will come with you," Michelle said. "I would like to share the rest of the gingersnap cookies with the other church members."

As soon as the missionaries left Pastor Emeka's house, Michelle said, "I feel so out of place here."

"Let's walk around the neighborhood and pray so that we can process our thoughts," Matthew said.

When the missionaries walked past the entrance of the church, they noticed a five-gallon plastic cooler with a broken lid sitting on the floor. It was full of rice, meat scraps and tiny pieces of vegetables. Most of the church members were sitting around the cooler, eating the meal with their hands, while others were using an assortment of plastic cups and sticks. A few of the church members had torn off pieces of a banana leaf that they were using as plates.

After noticing the desperation on many of the church members' faces, Michelle immediately opened her backpack and started distributing the gingersnap cookies. Beginning with the youngest children first and working her way up to the teenagers, she was able to give almost all the adults a package of cookies before running out.

"Are you ready to go on our prayer walk now?" Matthew asked.

"I don't know if I can pray," Michelle said as she followed Matthew outside. "I need a good, long venting session. This is so horrible, I don't have any words to describe what I'm feeling."

"If we are being called to do ministry here, I would much rather be inside the church, sitting on the floor and eating food out of the plastic cooler, than inside Pastor Emeka's house dining with all the important elders and leaders who only want to use us for money," Matthew said.

"When I saw them eating food out of that dirty

container, I could feel so much love and compassion for the poorest members of his congregation," Michelle said. "My heart broke when I saw that little old lady in the back and the crippled man near the window. These are the people that Jesus would be drawn to. He would rebuke the rich and powerful Pharisees for being greedy, and spend his time ministering to the poor and humble of heart."

"I'm wondering if the same dynamic exists in America and that we have been blinded from recognizing it all these years," Matthew said.

"What do you mean?" Michelle asked.

"In America, we have grown accustomed to the all-important priests, pastors and bishops who separate themselves from the rest of the congregation," Matthew said. "We have also grown accustomed to the famous Hollywood celebrities who separate themselves from the rest of society. The same dynamic is also occurring here, but what is so shocking is that from our standard of living, the church elders and leaders don't appear to be all that important or rich."

"Didn't the Apostle John rebuke one of the churches in the Book of Revelation that had a similar problem?" Michelle asked. "The leadership thought they were so wealthy and important that they didn't need anything, but in reality, they were 'wretched, pitiable, poor, blind, and naked.'"[14]

"I don't know how to deal with this situation," Matthew said. "Because we need to pay Pastor Emeka more money to finalize our outreach plans on Wednesday, we should probably start walking back to his house."

"Very well," Michelle said. "I would like to get back to the retreat center before it gets dark."

4th CHAPTER

When Wednesday morning arrived, the driver picked up the missionaries at the retreat center. After driving a short distance, he pulled into a gas station and said, "We need more petrol."

"We filled your tank on Sunday," Matthew said.

"It's a very long journey," the driver said. "If we run out of petrol, we will not be able to buy more for ourselves."

After Matthew agreed to add four thousand more shillings to his tank, he said to the driver, "You do realize that almost everybody in America owns their own car. Some people in America own two or three cars."

Because the driver remained silent, Matthew continued by saying, "Every car in America comes with a miles-per-gallon rating. In Kenya, you probably have a kilometer-per-liter rating. Because a Toyota Corolla will average around thirty miles per gallon, it means you can drive four hundred miles on one tank of gas.

"After we filled your tank completely full of gas

on Sunday, you should have been able to drive around six hundred kilometers. If you drove eighty kilometers per hour to get through Nairobi, and twelve kilometers per hour on the dirt roads, the total distance would be around a hundred kilometers. Even if we drove three hundred kilometers on Sunday, you should still have plenty of gas. So you either owe us some money, or you owe us more kilometers."

"I don't have any money," the driver said. "The journey is very long and we needed more petrol. Pastor Emeka told me you would pay all expenses."

After driving an hour through the center of Nairobi and another forty minutes to pass through a series of very rough dirt roads, the missionaries arrived at the outreach location. The small village consisted of thirty-two adobe huts with grass roofs. Children were playing with a soccer ball in the community courtyard, and the scent of burning wood lingered in the air.

When Matthew stepped out of the vehicle, he asked the driver, "Where is Pastor Emeka?"

"He had a business deal that needed attention this morning," the driver said. "He will be coming soon."

"How soon?" Matthew asked.

"This is our man-on-ground," the driver said, pointing toward a tall man who was walking toward the vehicle.

"My name is Mutombo," the man said. "The shade canopy for our church service is right over here."

"Where are all the people?" Matthew asked.

"They're coming," Mutombo said. "Please have a seat and we will begin very soon."

After the missionaries took a seat underneath the shade canopy, they watched Mutombo walk back to the car to discuss something with the driver.

After a long time had passed Matthew said, "I don't like this. There are only twenty plastic chairs in the audience, and I don't want to spend two hundred dollars to deliver the Gospel message to twenty Christians."

"Didn't Pastor Emeka say he would gather all the non-believers together for our outreach?" Michelle asked.

"I want to minister to the Muslims," Matthew said.

When Mutombo returned from his conversation with the driver, Matthew asked, "Are there any Muslims in the area?"

"They live on the other side of the highway," Mutombo said, pointing toward a small village about five hundred meters away.

"Are you telling me that the Christians live on this side of the highway, and the Muslims live in that village over there?" Matthew asked.

"We don't mix well together," Mutombo said.

"I would like to invite the Muslims to our outreach," Matthew said.

"I didn't bring my headscarf," Michelle said.

"Why don't you stay here and greet our guests when they arrive?" Matthew said. "I will run over there to invite the Muslims."

"I will come with you," Mutombo said.

After crossing the highway, Matthew and Mutombo noticed a group of men who were playing cards. Several of the men appeared to be gambling, and the rest of them were standing around watching.

"Just translate whatever I say into a language they can understand," Matthew said.

"I will speak to them in Swahili," Mutombo said.

When Matthew and Mutombo approached the men, they stopped playing and gave them their full attention. "My name is Matthew Goodwin and I would like to invite you to our outreach. I have an important message to share with you from the Quran."

After listening to Mutombo's translation, several men became agitated because Matthew's presence was interrupting their card game. When one of the men recognized Mutombo as the Christian evangelist who lived on the other side of the highway, he started screaming at the other men in an attempt to incite violence. Because Matthew and Mutombo had no idea what the man was saying, they stood there in silence, watching the men grow more angry and agitated.

After what seemed to be a very long time, Matthew said to the men, "Everybody who wants to hear what I have to say, please come over here."

Almost immediately, sixteen men left the card game and followed Matthew and Mutombo to a large tree that would provide enough shade for the meeting. After removing a notebook from his backpack, Matthew began by asking the men a simple question: "Why is the story about Noah and the great flood mentioned in the Quran so many times?"

Because nobody in the audience could answer the question, Matthew continued by saying, "The Quran mentions the story of Noah and the great flood in seven different chapters.[15] As you know, the entire seventy-first chapter is all about Noah and the great flood. So it would seem to me, if the Quran mentions the story of Noah in seven different chapters, then the message about the great flood must be very important."

After all the men agreed, Matthew continued by saying, "I'm sure everybody knows the story, but please allow me to read some of my favorite passages. In surah seven, God sent Noah to his people to deliver a warning.[16] In surah eleven, Noah said to the people of his generation, 'I am a plain warner unto you.'[17] The chieftains of the people disbelieved Noah and started mocking him. So we see in surah twenty-three how Noah received a commission to build a large ship.[18]

"After Allah sent the great flood, he said to Noah in surah fifty-four, 'See how dreadful was My punishment after My warnings!'[19] The question I would like to ask you today is: Why did Allah destroy the entire world with the great flood?"

"Because of sin and disobedience," one of the men said who was standing next to the tree.

"I like that answer because it would imply that the penalty for sin is death," Matthew said. "The reason why the story of Noah and the great flood is mentioned so many times in the Quran is that we are all sinners. If there is a man here today who has never sinned, please raise your hand."

Because nobody in the audience raised their hand, Matthew continued by saying, "Because we are all sinners, we all deserve the death penalty; but because Allah is kind and merciful, he has provided us with a remedy that's mentioned in the Quran eleven times. In eleven different passages, the Quran confirms that Jesus is the Messiah.[20]

"Now there was a point in my life when I didn't understand why Allah sent the Messiah. I didn't understand who the Messiah was and why the Messiah was important. At this point in my life, nothing seemed to be going right. It felt like my entire life was under the heavy curse of sin and disobedience. Has anyone ever felt that way? That nothing you seem to do ever works out right? Have you ever felt cut off and distant from God's great love and mercy?"

Because nobody responded, Matthew went on to say, "I remember one day picturing what would happen to me if I died and stood in front of Allah's throne on the Day of Judgment. All of my sin and disobedience was piled high upon my head. It was a very heavy load because I was a very bad sinner.

"When Allah looked at me, he was very angry. He said to me, 'The penalty for sin is death.' Because I deserved the death penalty, Allah had me arrested and put me in a prison cell. The bars on the jail cell door were very thick. It was cold and dark. As I awaited my execution, I remembered what the Quran said about the Messiah, so I asked Allah to send the Messiah to me.

"When the Messiah appeared, his presence illuminated the cold, dark jail cell with his mercy and grace. He opened the door and sat down next to me. Then the Messiah said to me, 'I will pay the death penalty on your behalf, you can now go free.'

"To accept the Messiah's sacrifice, I had to stand up and walk out of the jail cell. As soon as I accepted the Messiah's sacrifice on the cross for the forgiveness of my sins, the dark, heavy barrier of sin that separated me from God's love was instantly removed. I felt so free and blessed. The fullness of God's love could finally flow into my life.

"That's the prayer I would like to pray with you today, but the only problem is, I cannot pray this prayer on your behalf. This prayer is between your heart and God himself. I would be happy to lead and guide you in the same prayer that I prayed, but because the prayer is very serious, you will need to quiet your hearts and close your eyes. It may be helpful to picture what it would be like to stand in front of God's throne on the Day of Judgment."

* * *

When Draven realized the men were about to pray a prayer of salvation that would transition them out of the kingdom of darkness and into the kingdom of heaven, he said to the demonic spirits in the area, "Find a way to distract them. Cause an interruption. Create an emergency that needs everybody's attention."

* * *

After Matthew led twelve men in a prayer for salvation, he realized that he needed to get back across the highway. Because he felt a strong bond and connection with the men, he shook everybody's hand and said to his newfound friends, "I'm going to send you guys a fifty-kilo bag of rice because I want to bless you. I'm very sorry that I have to leave now, but by God's grace, I will come back to visit with you very soon."

"*Inshallah*," one of the men said as Matthew and Mutombo rushed back across the highway.

When Matthew and Mutombo returned to the shade canopy, more than fifty people were waiting for the service to begin. Because Michelle had been entertaining the guests for over an hour, she said, "Where did you guys go? I was starting to get worried. You also broke rule number three—that we should always stay together—then you leave me here all alone."

"I'm very sorry," Matthew said. "Please forgive me. I lost track of time. It will not happen again."

"What were you doing over there?" Michelle asked.

"It was a divine appointment," Matthew said. "There was a large group of men playing cards. After we interrupted their card game, one of the men started screaming at us, trying to incite the others to violence. I really thought we were dead. Thank God, Mutombo stood beside me, solid as a rock. If we would have taken off running, they would have hunted us down and beaten us to death."

"Then what happened?" Michelle asked.

"We spent the entire time ministering to the majority of the men," Matthew said. "Except for that one guy. Do you know what he was saying?"

"I don't know the language he was speaking," Mutombo said.

"Please don't be angry with me," Matthew said to Michelle, then he kissed her and approached the front of the shade canopy.

When the audience realized the service was about to begin, the lively conversations quieted down until all that remained was the sound of the gentle African breeze blowing through the tall native grass that surrounded the shade canopy. Matthew started his message by asking the audience a question: "How many people here today consider themselves to be Christian?"

Because everybody in the audience raised their hands, Matthew adjusted his message accordingly by saying, "I have a three-part process that I wanted to share with you that will empower you to work in partnership with God.

"This process is so simple that even a small child can understand how it works. The three parts of this process that will allow you to work in partnership with God are *surrender*, *listening* and *obedience*. Let's go over the parts very carefully, and then we will tie them together so that you can begin to work in partnership with God to accomplish great things with your life.

"The first part of the process is surrender. This occurs when we acknowledge Jesus as the Lord of our lives. There are many Bible passages where Jesus is called Lord.[21] If Jesus is truly our Lord and Master, then that would make us his obedient servants. If Jesus is truly the Lord of our lives, and if we are truly his obedient servants, then the next logical step in that servant-master relationship would be to find out what our Master wants us to be doing with our time, talent and resources.

"That's where the process of listening becomes very important. There are many Bible passages that speak about our need to listen.[22] In the Gospel of John, Jesus says, 'My sheep hear my voice. I know them, and they follow me.'[23] The process of hearing the Lord's voice would involve listening. After we ask the Lord questions about the direction of our lives, it's important to spend time in silence, listening for the Holy Spirit's answers.

"Once we hear the Lord speak to us in the quiet stillness of our hearts, we need to be obedient and follow through with whatever the Lord is calling us to do. Obedience is an essential part of the servant-master relationship and there are many Bible passages that speak about our need to be obedient.[24] Once we accomplish whatever the Lord is calling us to do, then we would start the process all over again.

"We would *surrender* our current situation to the Lord, ask questions about what we should be doing, and after spending time *listening* for the Lord's guidance, we would follow through with more *obedience*. So you see, this three-part process will allow you to work in partnership with the Lord to accomplish great things with your life."

After Matthew shared many personal examples of how the three-part process of surrender, listening and obedience had been a tremendous blessing in his own life, he concluded the service with prayer and promised to buy the villagers several bags of rice. After all the people left the meeting and went back to their homes, Matthew asked the driver, "Where is Pastor Emeka?"

"He's coming," the driver said. "He called me an hour ago and said he was being detained in traffic."

"Let's call him back," Matthew said. "Please tell Pastor Emeka that the service has ended and there's no need for him to make the journey all the way out here."

After making the phone call, the driver said, "Pastor Emeka wants us to wait for him here. He is coming very soon."

"Would you like a tour of the village while we are waiting?" Mutombo asked. "I would be happy to show you around."

"That would be great," Michelle said.

While the missionaries were taking a tour of the area, Matthew removed his travel wallet from his pocket and said, "I would like to thank you for setting up the outreach today. I was very happy with the turnout and I wanted to bless you with some money."

"I am so very blessed," Mutombo said.

"Here's four thousand shillings for the work you did today, and I also wanted to ask for your help to set up another outreach for the Muslims next week," Matthew said. "After our near-death experience this morning, I learned that Muslims and Christians don't mix well together. There's no way a devout Muslim man will ever attend a Christian event, so we will need to set up a totally Muslim event and only invite Muslims."

"I know a man from Eskange Town that works at a service station," Mutombo said. "Although he is a devout Muslim, I have had many spiritual conversations with him in the past. I think he would be willing to invite his friends and neighbors to his home for such an event."

"I think we should make the main focus of the meeting about helping the poor," Matthew said. "Please tell the man at the service station that you know an American businessman who wants to share a message from the Quran and distribute a fifty-kilo bag of rice to his neighbors for the purpose of blessing the poor. Then ask your friend if he has any specific needs in his community that we could help him fulfill."

"I think that approach would work," Mutombo said. "How could he refuse to help the poor?"

"It would be nice to have an assortment of candy treats," Michelle said. "That way, I would have something to give away to all the women and children. We will also need a roll of plastic bags, the kind they use at grocery stores, so we could put a two-pound serving of rice in everyone's bag."

"We also need to buy two bags of rice for the Christian village, and another bag for the Muslim village," Matthew said.

"I will visit the grain dealer tomorrow to inquire about the price," Mutombo said.

As the missionaries were discussing their outreach plans, Pastor Emeka arrived in a white Toyota hatchback. The driver appeared to be in a hurry and didn't slow down for the children who were playing in the courtyard. After making an abrupt U-turn, he parked his car near the shade canopy.

"Please give me your cell number and let's keep our future ministry plans private," Matthew said.

"Most certainly," Mutombo said. "I will contact my friend at the gas station and will not discuss the situation with anyone else."

As the missionaries approached the shade canopy, Pastor Emeka asked, "How was your outreach meeting? I was unable to attend because of all the problems I encountered this morning."

"The outreach was excellent," Michelle said. "We are very happy with the results."

"I had additional expenses with another driver this morning," Pastor Emeka said. "I was hoping we could settle accounts with the money you owe me."

"We agreed on twenty thousand shillings for the outreach," Matthew said. "I paid you six thousand shillings at the restaurant and another twelve thousand at your church. Then I paid seven thousand shillings to fill the tank with gas, and another four thousand shillings for gas a few days later. So the way I see it, you owe me money."

"The petrol is very expensive in Kenya," Pastor Emeka said. "I thought you would understand the hardships we are experiencing every day."

"We're learning the hard way," Michelle said.

"I am requesting that you pay me an additional ten thousand shillings for the second car that I needed to hire this morning," Pastor Emeka said.

"Thank you for showing us your church on Sunday," Michelle said. "I was blessed by the experience, but it's getting late. We are tired from all the work today, and we need to get back to the retreat center."

Because Pastor Emeka kept arguing with Matthew for more money, he gave him an additional six thousand shillings before joining Michelle, who was already sitting in the back seat of the car.

"Are they going to take us hostage until we pay more money?" Michelle asked.

"We could call Charles for a ride," Matthew said, "except I wouldn't know how to describe our location."

"Do we need to add another rule to our list about pastors who spend all their time sending emails to ministry websites begging for money?" Michelle asked.

"I learned another lesson the hard way," Matthew said. "This lesson was a lot cheaper than the ministry search function option, where we would have to pay two hundred dollars per day in advance."

After the missionaries started to pray, Overwatch sent an assignment of angels to bind up the demonic spirits of greed that were driving Pastor Emeka's behaviors. A few minutes later, the driver returned to the vehicle and said, "Pastor Emeka said that we should return to the retreat center straight away."

"Thank you," Michelle said. "It's getting late and we need to get back."

5th CHAPTER

The next day, Mutombo called and said, "I spoke to my friend Abdullah at the service station. He wanted to conduct an outreach to help his neighbors very early on Saturday morning. He wanted to start the meeting around seven o'clock because he needs to work that day. I told him we wouldn't be able to arrive that early, so we agreed on eight o'clock."

"How long will it take to get there?" Matthew asked.

"The roads are good in that area," Mutombo said. "From the retreat center, it should only take us fifty minutes."

"I will work on buying the supplies that we need," Matthew said. "Let's meet at the retreat center at seven o'clock in the morning."

* * *

When Draven learned about the outreach location, he entered a mosque in Abdullah's neighborhood, looking for assistance. When the commander of the mosque detected Draven's presence, he said, "Why have you come here?"

"I need your assistance," Draven said. "American missionaries are planning an outreach at Abdullah's house on Saturday morning, and we need to stop them."

"I will inform Dajjal the Destroyer," the demonic spirit said.

* * *

A few hours later, Mutombo called Matthew back and said, "Abdullah wants to change the meeting time to ten o'clock in the morning. I don't understand why because he originally needed to work at the service station on Saturday morning. I told him we would arrive at his home early to get everything set up. If the new time is okay with you, I will pick you up at eight o'clock in the morning."

"It's not a problem," Matthew said. "Michelle and I like getting up early and spending time in the chapel, so an extra hour of prayer will work out perfectly."

* * *

When Saturday morning arrived, the missionaries loaded three, twenty-five-kilo bags of rice in the back of a silver-colored Nissan Sentra, and then drove an hour to a remote location in the Mutuni District. For most of the journey, the roads were paved, but shortly after entering Abdullah's subdivision, their driver parked his car alongside a washed-out gully that contained several inches of muddy water.

"We need to leave the car here," Mutombo said.

As the driver and Mutombo were unloading the rice and placing the bags on their shoulders, Matthew said to Michelle, "Don't forget your headscarf."

"I have it right here," Michelle said, then she removed it from her daypack, placed it over her head and wrapped the edges around her neck.

After walking ten minutes, while carrying the bags of rice on their backs, the missionaries arrived at a small white house with a rust-colored metal roof. Several men were seated on chairs in the front yard, and at least twenty-five women were seated behind them on the ground.

As the missionaries approached the location, an older man who was standing beside the road greeted them by saying, "My name is Abdullah. You are most welcome here. This is my house and these are my neighbors."

Although the meeting time had been rescheduled for ten o'clock, because everybody was ready to start the service, Matthew took a list of Quran passages out of his daypack and said to the audience, "I would like to share with you the story about the destruction of Sodom and Gomorrah. The account is listed in the Quran in six different chapters.[25]

"I'm sure most of you know the story about how Allah sent two angelic messengers to warn Lot about the impending destruction. Allah wanted to destroy Sodom and Gomorrah because of their great wickedness. In surah seven, the Quran says that the people of Sodom and Gomorrah committed an 'abomination such as no creature ever did before.'[26] We know one of the abominable sins was homosexuality because the town's people wanted to have sex with the angelic messengers, but there were many other sins as well.

"Allah wanted to save Lot and his entire household, except for his wife. I find it very interesting, and I'm wondering what the women in the audience have to say about that. Why didn't Allah want to save Lot's wife? The Quran is very clear in surah fifteen where it says, 'Except his wife, of whom We had decreed that she should be of those who stay behind.'[27]

"Does anyone know why Allah wanted Lot's wife to perish along with the wicked?" Matthew asked.

After a long moment of silence, a woman who was sitting on the ground next to Michelle said, "Because she looked back."

"Very good answer," Matthew said. "We see in surah eleven where it says, 'Let not one of you turn round all save thy wife.'[28] That would indicate to me that even the smallest sin of disobedience deserves the death penalty. We also know from other passages in the Quran that the penalty for all forms of sin is death; even the smallest degree of sin deserves the death penalty.

"This reality is very concerning to me because we have all committed some kind of sin in our past. If there's a sinless person in the audience today, I would like for you to introduce yourself and share with us how you're able to live a sinless life."

Because nobody in the audience wanted to

introduce themselves as a sinless person, Matthew took another list of passages out of his daypack and said to the audience, "I would like to share with you a list of Allah's names that are mentioned in the Quran. These are more than just names because they describe Allah's nature and character.

"For example, in surah three, one of Allah's names is the Giver of Life.[29] This is not just a name, because God is the giver of life. We also see from surah nine that Allah is the Most Kind.[30] He is the Source of all Goodness, the Protector, the Loving One, the Provider, the Bestower of Peace, the Merciful and the Most Compassionate.[31]

"Because Allah is the Merciful and the Most Compassionate, he doesn't want to see anyone perish, but for all people to come to repentance. We also know from Sacred Scripture that God takes no pleasure in the death of the wicked but wants all people to turn away from their sins so that they may live.[32] So you see the dilemma that we are all facing. On one hand, we are all sinners and deserve the death penalty. On the other hand, God is merciful and compassionate and doesn't want to see anyone perish.

"The remedy for this dilemma that applies to all people has been described in the Quran eleven times.[33] Because Allah is merciful and compassionate, he sent the Messiah to pay the death penalty on our behalf. The Messiah is no ordinary man because in surah sixty-six, the Quran says, 'Mary, daughter of Imran, whose body was chaste, therefor We breathed therein something of

Our Spirit. And she put faith in the words of her Lord and His Scriptures, and was of the obedient.'[34]

"In addition to that passage, the Quran also confirms the virgin birth of the Messiah in surahs three, nineteen, and twenty-one.[35] Because Mary was a virgin, whose body was chaste, God breathed his Spirit into her body, allowing her to give birth to the Messiah. Not only did the Messiah come from a supernatural birth, but he also lived a supernatural life.

"We see in surah three that the Messiah had the ability to heal sick people and cleanse lepers of their disease.[36] We also see in surah five that the Messiah had the ability to restore sight to the blind and raise the dead to life.[37] The Messiah also experienced a supernatural death when he paid the penalty on the cross for the forgiveness of our sins.[38] The question that I wanted to ask you today is very simple: Have you accepted the Messiah's sacrifice on the cross of Calvary for the forgiveness of your sins?"

Because everybody in the audience remained silent, Matthew continued by saying, "We all have a choice to make: Because we are all sinners, we can pay the death penalty ourselves, or we can allow the Messiah to pay the death penalty on our behalf. What choice do you want to make? Do you want to reject the Messiah's sacrifice on the cross for the forgiveness of your sins, or do you want to accept the Messiah's gift of salvation?"

"We accept everything the Quran says about the Messiah," one man said.

"What about you?" Matthew asked as he pointed toward Abdullah.

"I want to accept the Messiah's sacrifice on the cross for the remission of my sins," Abdullah said.

Once Abdullah made a public acknowledgment, Matthew continued pointing to all the other members of the audience, asking every person the same question. After everybody in the audience gave a positive response, Matthew asked everybody to close their eyes and imagine what it would be like to stand in front of Allah's throne on the Day of Judgment.

After leading the audience in a prayer of salvation where they invited Jesus into the jail cell to pay the death penalty on their behalf, Matthew concluded the prayer by asking everyone to surrender their lives into God's service, so they could be filled with the Holy Spirit.

"Now that we have shared a spiritual blessing together, I would like to give everybody a bag of rice as our way of saying thank you for spending your time with us this morning," Matthew said.

As Michelle was handing every person in the audience a plastic bag, Mutombo and the driver moved the sacks of rice closer to the front of the line that was beginning to form. When Abdullah's wife realized the missionaries would need a serving container to distribute the rice in equal proportions, she brought out several different-sized containers from her house.

"Let's use this one," Matthew said, choosing a five-quart stainless steel mixing bowl. "It's the perfect size, because we don't want to run out."

After all the guests had received a large serving of rice, there was half a bag remaining, so Matthew carried it over to Abdullah and said, "Please keep the rest of the rice for yourself. I'm very grateful that we were able to use your property for the meeting. Thank you for inviting all your neighbors. I hope everybody was blessed by the service."

"Everybody was so very happy," Abdullah said. "Please come back anytime. You are most welcome here."

As the missionaries were getting ready to leave, two motorcycles stopped in front of Abdullah's house. One of the men was talking on his cell phone while the other man said to Matthew, "We will give you a ride. Climb on the back of our bikes."

"No, thank you," Michelle said. "It's a nice day and we would rather walk."

"We wanted to show you our mosque," the other man said. "We will take you there so you can meet our Imam."

After declining to get on the back of the motorcycles several times, the missionaries, Mutombo and the driver continued walking down the dirt road toward their vehicle. Several minutes later, they noticed two men approaching in the distance. One man was dressed in a white Islamic gown, and the other was wearing dress pants and a western-styled jacket. As the men approached, one of them started screaming in Swahili, *"Mkamateni mzungu! Mkamateni mzungu!"*

"What's going on?" Michelle asked.

"This is the Imam from the mosque," Mutombo explained. "The other man is a police officer. The Imam is angry because you didn't ask his permission. He is saying, 'Arrest him! Arrest him!'"

"What should we do?" Michelle asked.

"Keep walking back to the car," Mutombo said. "Don't get on the motorbikes or go to the mosque, because it's a trap."

As the missionaries continued walking back to the car, the police officer received a phone call and started walking slower until he eventually stopped on the side of the road. The angry Imam kept following the missionaries while Mutombo continued speaking to him in Swahili. Once they reached the vehicle, the driver unlocked the doors, everybody jumped inside, and they drove away.

"What was that all about?" Matthew asked as the driver and Mutombo continued a heated debate with each other in Swahili.

"We want to drop you off on the side of the road around the next corner," Mutombo said. "I don't know if you remember the military checkpoint we passed on the way here, but we are concerned the police officer has called the military checkpoint with instructions to stop our vehicle. The driver is concerned they will arrest everyone and confiscate his car. That's why we want to drop you off so you can hide in the bushes down there. Once we pass through the checkpoint, I will rent

another vehicle and come back to get you when everything is safe."

"We didn't do anything wrong," Michelle said.
"It was an excellent outreach, and everybody was very
happy."

"The government in Kenya honors Sharia law,"
Mutombo said. "We have special courts that handle
those cases. If you had gotten on the back of the bikes
and been taken inside the confines of the mosque, the
Imam would have the right to arrest you and prosecute
you under Sharia law. I'm sure the Imam would accuse
you of breaking the most serious of all Islamic laws and
they would hold you in detention until the outcome of
the trial. Because the Imam was so very angry, I'm sure
they would have found you guilty on all the charges."

After the driver pulled over on the side of the road,
Mutombo said, "Please wait behind those bushes down
there and stay out of sight. I will come back in about an
hour with a different vehicle to pick you up."

After the missionaries walked down a gently sloping
hillside, they took a seat on a rock outcrop that was surrounded by tall native grasses. It was the perfect hiding
location because it was hidden behind several bushes and
facing the sun.

"Would you like some gingersnap cookies?"
Michelle asked. "I also have an extra bag of caramel
candies that I found hiding in my daypack."

"I'm very sorry," Matthew said, removing a bottle
of water from his daypack. "I promised your mother we

wouldn't do anything stupid or dangerous, and here we are, hiding in the bushes from the cops."

"I thought the outreach was excellent," Michelle said. "Those people were so kind and humble. The response to your message was outstanding. It can only be explained by divine intervention. It was truly miraculous to see how they accepted the Gospel message with such open hearts."

"Do you remember how Abdullah wanted the meeting time set up at eight o'clock in the morning because he needed to work at the service station?" Matthew asked. "Then Mutombo called back a few hours later and wanted to change the meeting time to ten o'clock. I'm thinking the time change occurred after the Imam found out about the meeting. He probably wasn't able to attend the earlier time, so he wanted the meeting moved back several hours so he could have us arrested."

"Do you think Abdullah set us up?" Michelle asked.

"I don't think Abdullah was involved, because all of his neighbors were ready and waiting for us when we arrived," Matthew said. "I'm thinking it was divine intervention that we were able to arrive early and finish the event before the Imam could get there."

"How do you think the Imam found out about the outreach?" Michelle asked.

"I'm not sure," Matthew said. "Maybe Abdullah called him, hoping he would help advertise the event; or maybe Abdullah was hoping the Imam would invite the poor Muslims in the community to the outreach.

One thing I know for sure is that after the Imam learned about the event, he naturally assumed it was a Christian outreach, because if it were authentically Muslim, we would have brought our financial gifts directly to the mosque for the official Islamic leadership to distribute amongst themselves."

"It's too bad the Imam couldn't get to our event any sooner," Michelle said, "because he missed out on a free bag of rice."

* * *

After the missionaries spent an hour talking, praying and eating gingersnap cookies on the sunny hillside overlooking the lush countryside, a white delivery van stopped on the side of the road and began sounding its horn. When the missionaries reached the vehicle, Mutombo said, "There were no issues at the military checkpoint. We were able to pass directly through without any problems."

"Thank you for protecting our safety," Matthew said. "How much do we owe you for the additional vehicle?"

"Let's discuss the additional expenses and financial compensation in private," Mutombo said.

When the missionaries reached the retreat center, Michelle waited in the lobby while Matthew negotiated a price with Mutombo. The conversation appeared to be growing more hostile as time passed, but eventually, Matthew removed his travel wallet from his pocket and paid Mutombo twelve thousand shillings to cover the cost of both vehicles, along with an additional bonus to help compensate him for the risk of being arrested.

When Matthew entered the retreat center lobby, Michelle asked, "How much did that cost us?"

"I paid him what he wanted and even gave him a bonus," Matthew said, "but I don't think we are going to work with Mutombo in the future."

"Let's walk over to the store and prepare a nice dinner for ourselves tonight," Michelle said. "I would like to spend the evening in the chapel praying to see what the Lord wants us to do next."

* * *

After dinner, when the missionaries entered the chapel, Matthew knelt down in front of the tabernacle on the right side, while Michelle knelt in the front row on the left side. Although the interior lights inside the chapel had been turned off at night, there was still enough exterior light from the retreat center building filtering through the stained glass windows to create a peaceful, inner glow inside the chapel, so that the missionaries could see what they were doing without using their flashlights.

After praying for over an hour, Matthew moved over, sat down next to Michelle and said, "I'm not hearing anything from the Lord except for the word *proceed*. I don't think we were in any real danger today. I'm still feeling peace in my heart, although, I'm not sure what to do next or how we should proceed."

"I think we should visit Kibera tomorrow," Michelle

said. "I have been reading articles on the Internet and it is the most interesting place because the word *kibera* means jungle. Many years ago, when the British were colonizing Kenya, the soldiers used to camp out in the jungle. It soon became a place for homeless people, and today, it's two miles long and a half-mile wide.

"The Kenyan government considers Kibera an unauthorized settlement and refuses to provide water, sewer or electricity to any of the residents. It is the largest slum in Africa, with an estimated population of three hundred thousand people. It's also the most culturally diverse and vibrant community in all of Kenya.

"What I found so interesting is that when the Kenyan government built nicer apartment buildings for the residents who live there, some of the people would sublease the apartments to middle-class citizens, then move back to Kibera because they enjoyed living in such a vibrant community. There are even some people who have good jobs in Nairobi, but they choose to live in Kibera because they want to save money on rent.

"Because the Kenyan government considers Kibera an unauthorized settlement, the residents have no legal rights of land ownership, so they build small shacks out of sticks, mud and sheets of tin. There are very few main roads where vehicles can pass. It's mostly tiny shacks built on top of each other with a maze of walking paths between the houses. Many of the women who live there open up small shops and sell every kind of product imaginable on the sides of the main roads.

"It's possible to rent a hundred and twenty square foot structure with a dirt floor for ten dollars per month. The only problem is that six people live inside those tiny shacks, and there's no running water and very few public bathroom facilities. The people who live in Kibera call the restroom facilities *flying toilets*, because after doing their business in a plastic sack, they need to dispose of the waste somewhere, so they throw it in a huge pile with all the other garbage.

"Because of the open sewers and trash everywhere, deadly diseases—including cholera, typhoid and tuberculosis—are out of control. Crimes such as rape, murder and robbery are common occurrences. In addition to all the other lawlessness, Kibera has a fifty percent unemployment rate, and only forty percent of the children attend school."

"That sounds like the place where Jesus would spend most of his time," Matthew said. "He would denounce the religious leaders for hiding out in their prestigious sanctuaries and venture deep into the heart of Kibera, healing the sick, casting out demons and proclaiming the good news."

6th CHAPTER

The following morning, after the missionaries made peanut butter and banana sandwiches for breakfast, they approached a group of motorcycle taxi drivers to inquire about a ride to Kibera.

"Let's find a spirit-filled Christian driver," Michelle said as she pointed toward a young man with a happy, peaceful glow on his face.

After Matthew inquired about the price, the young man said, "It depends on what part of Kibera because the slum continues for several kilometers. Many of the pathways are impassable, even for a motorbike. If you want a ride to the main entrance, the price is fifty bob."

"How much is fifty bob?" Michelle asked.

"I think it means fifty coins," Matthew said.

"We would like a tour of Kibera," Michelle said. "Before we negotiate a price, I want to know if you are a Christian or a Muslim."

"I'm a Christian," the young man said. "My name is Samuel, and I attend the African Inland Church."

"How about we give you five hundred bobs, and you drive us all around Kibera, giving us a tour of everything?" Matthew asked.

"Then you bring us back here when we are finished with the tour," Michelle said.

"Most certainly, I will do that," the young man said.

"Let me put on my headscarf so that the wind doesn't whip my hair around into a big mess," Michelle said.

"We should also wear our sunglasses for eye protection," Matthew said, opening up his daypack.

After the missionaries climbed on the back of Samuel's motorcycle, he passed through the Koto-Bobby Junction and drove down several side streets before entering the slum.

"I didn't realize we were this close," Matthew said.

A few minutes later, Samuel pulled over to show the missionaries Karanja Road, which was lined with small shops constructed out of corrugated tin sheets, wooden poles, sticks and scraps of plastic that were used to patch large holes in the sides of the buildings.

"I'm seeing a lot of potential here," Michelle said. "It would be very easy to draw a large crowd of people."

"We would need to hire several security guards," Matthew said. "If we tried distributing a bag of rice on the side of the road, a huge crowd would form. People would be fighting, pushing and trampling each other to get whatever they could before we ran out."

After Samuel showed the missionaries the Nairobi

River that ran alongside Kibera, and the huge piles of trash that lined its banks, he turned down Jambo Road to show them more dilapidated shacks that had been plastered with adobe mud that people were using for their homes and businesses.

When Samuel stopped to show the missionaries the railroad tracks that ran through the heart of Kibera, Michelle asked, "Are there any churches in the area?"

"There are several churches in Kibera," Samuel said. "The African Inland Church is here, and also the Catholic Church."

"That would never work," Matthew said. "Muslims would never set foot inside a Christian church. Are there any mosques in the area?"

"There are several mosques in Kibera," Samuel said.

"What about a community center?" Michelle asked. "We are looking for a public meeting hall where both Muslims and Christians would feel comfortable gathering for a community meeting."

"The only place like that is the Salvation Army Center," Samuel said. "It's located outside the slum in the Kianda District, but everybody who lives around here knows how to find it."

"Will you please take us there?" Michelle asked.

"Most certainly," Samuel said.

When the missionaries arrived at the Salvation Army Center, they were greeted by a security guard who was stationed in a wooden shack behind the front gate.

"Where's the main office?" Matthew asked.

"I will show you," the security guard said. "If you want to bring your motorbike into the courtyard, I will open the gate for you."

"It's not necessary," Matthew said. "We wanted to see your public meeting hall to inquire about the rent."

"I can show you the meeting hall," the security guard said. "It can accommodate three hundred people and rents for eight thousand shillings per day."

"Does it come with sound equipment?" Michelle asked.

"The sound equipment costs an additional two

thousand shillings per day," the security guard said as he opened the front doors to show the missionaries the interior.

"It's very nice in here," Matthew said, looking around at the wide-open space.

"The stage is the perfect height for an audience of this size," Michelle said as she walked over to inspect several columns of white plastic chairs that had been stacked against the wall.

"We also provide catering services," the security guard said.

"Thank you for showing us around," Michelle said as they walked back outside.

"We could probably conduct three services per day here," Matthew said. "If three hundred people attended each service, we could deliver the Gospel message to nine hundred people per day. The only problem with ministering to that many people is the cost of the rice. If we gave every person a two-pound serving of rice, we would need eighteen hundred pounds of rice, which would cost more than eight hundred dollars per day. At that rate, we would run out of money in ten days."

"I'm wondering if we could create a seminar that's so dynamic and transforming that people would come to our event just for the information," Michelle said.

"What kind of seminar were you thinking about?" Matthew asked.

"Do you remember when Chaplain Hemingway told us that his best sermon ideas came from the times he spent interacting with the homeless population?" Michelle asked.

"I remember," Matthew said.

"When I saw those little kids sitting in front of the gate playing in the dirt, I wanted to reach into their lives with a message of personal empowerment," Michelle said. "We need a message about the transforming power of God that includes a vision of hope for the future, along with the motivation they need to rise above the crime, poverty and darkness that they are surrounded by every day."

"I would like to attend that event myself," Matthew said. "Do you think we can fill the conference hall three times per day without offering our guests any kind of tangible gifts to help compensate them for their time?"

"Maybe we can use the rice for our grand opening week," Michelle said. "It would be helpful for our guests to receive a nice present in exchange for helping us advertise our future events. Once we get our personal empowerment conference up and running, we could start cutting back on the rice. If we employed an effective marketing strategy, we should be able to fill the conference hall three times per day without any problems."

"I can't wait to hear about your marketing strategy," Matthew said. "Let's get back to the retreat center so we can get to work."

* * *

Later that evening, when the missionaries were spending time praying in the chapel that was illuminated by the soft glow of the stained glass windows, Matthew moved across the aisle to sit next to Michelle.

After a moment of silence, he said, "I think we should call the conference the Economic Empowerment Seminar, or maybe the Financial Empowerment Seminar. I'm not sure which term the people in Kenya use to describe their personal finances, but because everybody in the world is interested in money, it has the potential to attract the greatest amount of people."

"That's an excellent idea," Michelle said. "When I was in college, I attended a political rally and found myself fascinated by the marketing strategy they were using. The political rally was being held in a public park, but you needed a ticket to enter this free event.

"It was a unique marketing strategy that incorporated elements of crowd control. Even though it was a free event, the tickets added value to the venue because you needed one to enter. There were statements printed on the tickets in small font that said, 'Admission for one person' and 'Tickets are complimentary and not for re-sale.' The fine print also stated, 'Tickets are required but do not guarantee admission.'

"All the tickets contained the event's name, address and directions to the location, along with the time and date, so that tiny piece of paper, the size of a dollar bill, served as a form of advertising. If the park where the political rally was being conducted only held two thousand people, the organizers might print eighteen hundred tickets. That way, five thousand people wouldn't show up at an event designed to accommodate a smaller audience."

"Why do you think there was fine print that said, 'Tickets are required but do not guarantee admission'?" Matthew asked.

"It was a way for the organizers to control who attended the event," Michelle said. "If it was a Republican political rally, they wouldn't want ten thousand Democratic activists storming the gates and causing problems. They would probably want a strong base of seventy percent Republican voters with a mix of thirty percent swing voters.

"In our situation, we would probably want seventy percent Muslims and thirty percent Christians. We would want to print the meeting time and duration of the seminar on each ticket so that our guests would know what to expect. For example, we could print a statement on every ticket that said, 'This two-hour seminar begins at nine o'clock and concludes at eleven o'clock in the morning.'

"If the conference hall only holds three hundred people, we could print three hundred tickets and see how many people would show up. If only two hundred people showed up, we could print four or five hundred tickets for the following week. That way, the conference hall would be full for each session.

"We could also use the tickets as a way to control who is allowed to enter our audience. If we wanted to target Muslims, we would distribute the majority of the tickets at the mosque. If we wanted to invite Christians, we would distribute the tickets inside churches. We could also walk around the neighborhood and talk with residents and business owners to invite non-believers.

"It would also be nice if we used colored paper so that our tickets looked very official. If we included an official stamp or serial numbering system, the tickets would be difficult to copy, making them appear even more valuable."

"I'm wondering if we could use the green and white border design from an American dollar bill," Matthew said. "That way, when we pass out tickets for our Economic Empowerment Seminar, it would feel as if the recipients were already receiving something of value."

"I will start working on the design right away," Michelle said. "We are going to need a rental agreement from the Salvation Army Center before we print the dates and times on the tickets. I don't want to distribute any tickets unless we have an agreement in writing."

"Let's rent the building tomorrow morning," Matthew said. "I was thinking we should start with two seminars per day, on Monday, Wednesday and Friday. Then if everything goes well, we could rent the building for another week to see if it would be possible to conduct three seminars per day. I also want to give out rice on the first week for our grand opening, so that our guests will help us advertise future conferences. I think it's important that we make a good impression on the community so that our reputation grows."

"I think two seminars per day is a good idea, because it will give me more time to interact with all our guests," Michelle said. "I wanted to compile a database with everybody's names, cell numbers and email addresses so that we could send their friends and family members tickets for our future events."

*   *   *

After the missionaries rented the Salvation Army Center, Michelle printed eighteen hundred tickets that were the same size, shape and color as the American dollar bill. During this time, Matthew negotiated with the local grain dealers to acquire the lowest possible price on thirty-six bags of rice. After the majority of the tickets had been distributed and received with great joy at the local mosques, the rest of the tickets were distributed to the residents who lived in the area.

*   *   *

When Draven saw how many tickets the missionaries had distributed, he softened his shadow-stalking appearance and began searching the dilapidated structures in the center of Kibera, looking for the leader of the demonic principality that controlled that section of the city. He was immediately captured and taken to Revenga-Mortis, who knocked him to the ground and said, "All trespassers will be immediately executed upon entering my domain without my permission."

"I have permission from Dragon-Claw to operate in this area," Draven said. "I only seek to warn you about two missionaries from America."

"You have no authority here," Revenga-Mortis said.

"I am at your service," Draven said. "What do you want your servant to do?"

"We don't need your warnings or your interference," Revenga-Mortis said. "If the missionaries disrupt our operations, we will extinguish them ourselves."

"I will stay out of your territory," Draven said as he slowly backed away.

7th CHAPTER

On the day of the conference, after the meeting hall was filled to capacity, Matthew began his message by saying, "Welcome to the Economic Empowerment Seminar. My name is Matthew Goodwin, and I wanted to ask you a question about what makes America so successful.

"I'm not sure if you are familiar with American history, but Christopher Columbus sailed from Europe to discover the Americas less than six hundred years ago. We signed our Declaration of Independence in 1776, so technically, America is less than three hundred years old. In the last three hundred years, Americans have built all of our houses, roads, buildings, highways, bridges and infrastructure.

"There are also many inventions that have been discovered in America. For example, the light bulbs used to illuminate this meeting hall were invented in America. Everything from the laptop computer and cellular phone to the satellites that orbit our earth were all invented in

America. I can give you a long list of everything from the automobile to the airplane, along with the nuclear-powered submarine, that were all invented in America.

"Now I want you to compare all the success that Americans have experienced within the last three hundred years to all the poverty that people are experiencing in Africa. We know from history that people have been living in Africa for more than five thousand years. So I found myself wondering how could that be possible. How can Americans obtain so much success within the past three hundred years, while people in Africa have been living in so much poverty for more than five thousand years?"

Because nobody in the audience made a sound, Matthew went on to say, "This is the part of the seminar that requires audience interaction. There are no right or wrong answers. America has many problems, and I'm not saying that Americans are perfect; but how do you explain so much success in three hundred years and so much poverty after five thousand years?"

"Because we don't have any money," one man said.

"That's a good answer," Matthew said. "The lack of money. What else?"

"Tribalism," another man said.

"That's another good answer," Matthew said. "I'm assuming tribalism is where one tribe fights against another tribe. In America, we would call that a civil war. If half the country was constantly fighting with the other half of the country, it would destroy the entire nation. If half the population was constantly trying to oppress the other half of the population, it would harm the entire nation's ability to be productive. The opposite of attacking and destroying each other would be cooperation. In America, we want to see our neighbors be successful, so we are always supporting and encouraging each other."

"In Africa, we are always withholding information and trying to oppress our neighbors," another man said.

"Another issue that I have noticed in Africa is two different time zones," Matthew said. "The Nairobi airport operates on European time, while everybody else seems to operate on African time. Just imagine what would happen if an airplane was scheduled to depart at ten o'clock in the morning and one passenger was three hours late. That one person would have the ability to inconvenience all the other passengers on that plane. I realize this may seem like a small issue, but it adds up very quickly. If there were two hundred people on that plane that was delayed for three hours, that would add up to six hundred hours of non-productive downtime.

"Now multiply that by an entire nation. If every person in Kenya spent half the day sitting around for three hours waiting for someone to arrive, then all those people would be unproductive. They wouldn't be building better houses, businesses, roads, highways and infrastructure.

"It's a great offense in America if someone is more than ten minutes late without calling to let the other person know. I'm bringing this to your attention because it is something you can change immediately. You can make a commitment today to start respecting other people's time. When you start respecting other people's time, people will start treating you differently. Let me give you an example of how this works. Let's say there's a young man who wants to conduct business with me. If he's always running late and making excuses, I will learn not to trust anything he says, and I will not want to conduct business with him.

"If the young man is always on time, I will view him as a man of his word who can be trusted. If the young man respects me and my time, I will extend the same amount of respect to him. If the young man says ten o'clock in the morning and shows up at two o'clock in the afternoon, then starts making all kinds of excuses, I will not want to deal with him. I'm bringing this to your attention because it's something you can apply to your life immediately.

"Let me ask you another question: How many people in the audience have a goal to accomplish something in the next six months?"

Because nobody in the audience raised their hands or said anything, Matthew walked over to the chalkboard that was positioned in the center of the stage and said, "Let me show you how goals work."

After drawing an image that resembled a staircase on the chalkboard, he said, "Goals work like a set of stairs because they require a step-by-step plan. Nobody can jump from the bottom landing to the top landing in one step, but everybody can accomplish his or her goals if you can create a step-by-step plan to get from the bottom landing to the top landing.

"Goals also require a timetable. Without a time frame, goals are nothing more than hopes and dreams that may never materialize in the future. Without a step-by-step plan and a solid time frame, most people usually drift through life without accomplishing anything.

"Let me give you an example of how goals work using a staircase with five simple steps. I have a friend named Nicole who wants to start a ministry program, but she needs twelve hundred dollars to fund the project, so I'm going to write the letter G on the top landing. On the fourth step, I'm going to draw a dollar sign, which would represent the money needed to accomplish her goal. The question is: Where is Nicole going to get the money?

"During her prayer time, Nicole gets the idea of raising money on a website, so let me draw the letter W on the third step. Before Nicole can post her content on a fundraising website, she is going to need some text and images. So I will draw the letter T on the second step and the letter I on the first step.

"Goals also work in combination with a list of things to do. How many people in the audience have a list of things to do?"

Because only two people raised their hands, Matthew went on to say, "I have a list of things to do, and I'm constantly looking at my list to see what things

I could accomplish today to be more productive. When I accomplish an item, I cross it off the list and allow myself to feel good for being productive. I'm always adding new items to my list, and I'm constantly working hard to accomplish those tasks so that I can cross them off the list.

"In Nicole's situation, she wants to accomplish her goal within the next three months, so I'm going to draw a timeline underneath the staircase on the chalkboard. Every day, Nicole looks at her list of things to do, and she realizes her need to find the perfect images and start writing the text. The only problem is that Nicole is very busy, so she begins to procrastinate. Every day, when Nicole looks at her list of things to do, she feels tremendous pressure from the time frame because she wants to accomplish her goal in three months, and four weeks have already passed.

"Then one day Nicole has some free time and she starts researching the Internet. She finds the perfect images and starts writing the text. When she does, her creative abilities become engaged in the project and she gets very excited. After Nicole posts the images and text on the fundraising website, people from all over Europe start sending her small donations. Within a few short months, Nicole was able to raise the money she needed to accomplish her goal.

"Now that I have shown you how goals work, can anybody in the audience think of a reason why you wouldn't be able to accomplish your goals?"

"We don't have any money," one woman said.

"A lot of people from Africa don't have a formal education," another man said.

"Let me address both of those concerns," Matthew said. "In Nicole's situation, we can see that the money only flows once she starts the work. Before Nicole can raise the money on step number four, she needs to accomplish the work on the other steps leading up to that point.

"Let me give you an example of how the money will flow once you start the work. I have a friend named Kevin who wants to help the youth. Kevin has enough time and money to start helping the youth right away, but instead of starting the work, he wants to look for investors. He wants to apply for grants and spend all his time looking for a rich man who will give him the money. The problem with this approach is that Kevin has nothing to show the rich man. He hasn't helped a single person; he only wants money.

"After receiving a stack of rejection letters, Kevin became very discouraged and wanted to quit, so I said to my friend, 'You have enough time and money to start helping the youth today.' If Kevin would just start small with the resources he has, he may make many mistakes; but by learning from his mistakes, he would eventually get very good at helping the youth, and one day he would become very successful.

"As soon as Kevin is successful at helping the youth, that's when parents are going to get very interested in what he's doing. When that happens, the money will start flowing. The money will never flow unless you start the work.

"In regards to the other concern—about how the lack of formal education would prevent a person from accomplishing his or her goals—I would like to give you an example of two automobile mechanics. One man has the finest education that money can buy. He has a master's degree in auto mechanics and has read every car repair manual on the face of the planet, but he has never once fixed a car.

"The other man has no formal education; he learns by doing. He started with a small box of tools in a junkyard taking apart wrecked cars and putting them back together again. I'm sure he has made many mistakes along the way, but he always learns from his mistakes, and he has become an excellent auto mechanic.

"So let me ask you a question: If your car broke down, which mechanic would you want to hire? Would you hire the mechanic with no formal education or the mechanic with a master's degree?"

"The mechanic with no formal education," many people in the audience said with one accord.

"It doesn't cost any money for you to create a step-by-step plan to accomplish your goals," Matthew said. "If you can afford a piece of paper, you can make a list of things to do, and then you can draft a step-by-step plan to accomplish anything you want. If there's anyone in the audience who feels they need a little extra support to accomplish their goals, I would like to share with you a simple three-part process that will allow you to work in partnership with God to accomplish your goals.

"I realize there are many different religious backgrounds that are represented in the audience today, but this simple, three-part process applies to everybody, because God created all of us with a specific purpose and plan for our lives.[39] Because the step-by-step process of accomplishing goals will work for anyone, I would like for you to imagine the unlimited power and potential you can access if you start working in partnership with God to accomplish your goals.

"Think about that for a minute and ask yourself a simple question: Is there anyone more powerful than God? We have an all-powerful, loving God who created us with a specific purpose and plan for our lives. When you start working in partnership with God to accomplish his purpose and plan in your life, you will be unstoppable.

"The three-part process that will allow you to work in partnership with God to accomplish your goals is contained in both the Christian Bible and the Quran. So let me start with a Scripture passage for any Christians who may be present in the audience today.

"In the Gospel of Luke, Jesus says, 'Why do you call me "Lord, Lord," and do not do what I tell you?'[40] The word *lord* would imply that Jesus is your master and that you are his obedient servants. In this verse, Jesus is asking his servants: Why do you call me your Lord and

Master, and then run around all day long doing anything you want? Those same people will come back into the Lord's house after running around all day long, doing whatever they want, and call him Lord and Master, yet they have no desire to accomplish his will in their lives.

"Muslims may have a greater understanding in this area, because the definition of the word *Muslim* means a surrendered servant of Allah. According to the Quran in surah three, 'Religion with Allah is the Surrender to His will and guidance.'[41]

"The part I wanted to highlight in that passage is God's will and guidance. Before we can become surrendered servants, we have to be open to asking God questions about our lives and listening for his answers. The Christian Bible makes the same point in the Gospel of John where Jesus says, 'My sheep hear my voice. I know them, and they follow me.'[42]

"If the first part of this process is surrender, then the second part of the process is asking God questions about the direction of our lives. Once we ask questions and spend time in silence listening for the answers, the third part of the process is obedience. It's so simple that a small child can understand how it works. First we surrender our lives into God's service, then we spend time asking God questions and listening for the answers. Once we receive the answers, we need to proceed forth in obedience to accomplish everything that God is asking us to do.

"Now let's take this simple three-part process and

combine it together with what we learned earlier in creating goals. If you and God started working together to create your goals, then surely God is going to work in partnership with you to help you accomplish your goals. When you start working in partnership with God to accomplish what God is calling you to do, you will be unstoppable. Do you see the power in what I am sharing with you?"

Because everybody in the audience gave a positive response, Matthew went on to say, "Can anyone think of anything that would prevent God from working in partnership with you to accomplish your goals?"

Because nobody in the audience said anything, Matthew continued by saying, "I can think of one thing, and that is sin. Our sinful nature has the ability to separate us from God. Sin creates a barrier between humanity and God so that God's abundant blessings will not flow into our lives. I remember a point in my life when I was totally cut off from God because of all my sins.

"I used to be a very bad sinner. Then one day, I pictured what would happen if I died and stood in front of Allah's throne on the Day of Judgment. Allah was very angry with me. All my sins were piled high upon my head. It was a very heavy load, and I could see all the faces of the people I had hurt. Then in his anger, Allah sentenced me to death. Allah locked me up in a cold, dark prison cell.

"While I was awaiting my execution, I remembered what the Quran said about the Messiah. The

Quran mentions the Messiah eleven times.[43] In surah twenty-one, the Quran describes how Allah breathed his Spirit into Mary's body, and after she gave birth to the Messiah, Allah made her Son a token for all peoples.[44] In surahs three and five, the Quran describes how the Messiah lived a supernatural life by performing many miracles.[45] Because the Messiah also experienced a supernatural death, I asked Allah to send the Messiah to me so that he could pay the death penalty on my behalf.

"I pictured the Messiah coming to me in the prison cell. He opened the cell door and sat down next to me. He said to me, 'I will pay the death penalty on your behalf. You can now go free.'

"To accept the Messiah's sacrifice, I needed to stand up and walk out of the jail cell a free man. As soon as I accepted the Messiah's sacrifice on the cross for the forgiveness of my sins, the barrier that separated me from God was instantly removed. God's wisdom, guidance and blessings could flow freely into my life. It was such a powerful experience that I would like to pray the same prayer with you today.

"I can't pray this prayer on your behalf because it's between your heart and God himself. So if you are ready to pray, please close your eyes, and picture what it would be like to stand in front of God's throne on the Day of Judgment."

After Matthew led the audience in a prayer for salvation, he said, "Now that I have shared with you a spiritual blessing, we would like to give everybody in the audience a gift of appreciation for spending your valuable time with us. If you would like to invite your friends and family members to the seminars that we will be conducting next week, please make sure you give Michelle your name and phone number so we can send your friends and family members some free tickets."

After the missionaries gave everybody in the audience a plastic bag, they invited their guests to depart the building in a single-file line, so everyone could receive a serving of rice as they left the building. After all the rice had been distributed, many of the guests returned to the conference hall because they wanted to speak with Matthew and express their appreciation for the conference. While Matthew was greeting a large gathering, Michelle was surrounded by a group of people in the courtyard who wanted to sign up to receive free tickets for future conferences.

After the missionaries spent several hours greeting all the guests, they didn't have time to eat lunch because another large group of people who held tickets for the afternoon service began arriving that needed their attention. After Matthew delivered the same message to the afternoon audience, the missionaries spent several more hours personally connecting with all the guests in an attempt to make sure everybody felt welcomed and appreciated.

At the end of a very long day, Michelle said, "Although everybody loved your message, I don't think we should try to schedule three conferences in one day."

"I'm very happy with the turnout," Matthew said. "You did an excellent job with the marketing strategy, ticket design and distribution."

* * *

Several months later, after the missionaries had conducted twenty-two more Economic Empowerment Seminars, Michelle said, "Don't look directly at them, but do you see those angry-looking Muslim men standing outside the front gate near that building?"

"I see them," Matthew said.

"They were out there watching us last week, and I'm starting to get a very uneasy feeling," Michelle said.

"That's what I like about the Salvation Army Center," Matthew said. "We have the legal right to enter this property through our lease agreement. The exterior walls that surround this property offer us a lot of protection. We even have our own security guard. So if an angry Imam enters this property and causes us any problems, we could call the police and have him arrested."

"What would happen if they followed us back to the retreat center?" Michelle asked.

"Are you thinking we have overextended our stay in Kibera?" Matthew asked.

"The size of our audience is starting to dwindle, even though we have increased the amount of ticket distribution," Michelle said. "In addition, we are out of rice and running low on money, so this may be a good time to reevaluate our ministry objectives."

"Let's pray about it tonight," Matthew said. "If the Lord is calling us to move to a different location, I will terminate our lease agreement when the office opens first thing tomorrow morning."

8th CHAPTER

Later that evening, when the missionaries entered the dimly lit chapel, Matthew began walking back and forth as he offered his praise and worship to God. While he was pacing back and forth in the rear of the chapel, Michelle took a seat in the front row near the tabernacle. After ten minutes had passed, Matthew took a seat next to Michelle, closed his eyes and started practicing a contemplative form of prayer.

After twenty minutes had passed, Michelle leaned over and said, "I think we have overextended our stay in Kibera and we need a change of venue. In addition, my mother sent me an email last night about a Muslim man who converted to Christianity after he tried to poison a group of missionaries in Nigeria."

"What happened to the missionaries?" Matthew asked.

"The Muslim man was only pretending to be interested in Christianity because he wanted to invite the missionaries over to his house with the intention of putting poison in their food," Michelle said. "After the missionaries ate the meal, and the Muslim man realized that God had protected them from getting sick, he had a conversion experience. Shortly after telling his Imam what happened, he started reading the Bible. About a year later, he gave his life to Christ and was baptized."

"During my prayer time, I was asking the Lord some simple questions," Matthew said. "The first question that I asked was: Do you want us to conduct more Economic Empowerment Seminars at the Salvation Army Center? After meditating on the Lord's answer, I felt him say, 'No.' The next question that I asked was: Do you want us to leave Kibera? After meditating on the Lord's answer, I felt him say, 'Yes.'

"The next question I asked was: Where do you want us to go? After meditating on the Lord's answer for a very long time, I'm thinking we should book a flight to Kisumu to visit Pastor Thompson."

"Who's Pastor Thompson?" Michelle asked.

"He was a referral from the Anglican pastor that we met when we first arrived in Nairobi," Matthew said. "I have been communicating with him through email, and from everything he has written, he sounds like a very honest, humble and Godly man."

"Why do you say that?" Michelle asked.

"He lives in a remote farming area, and he built his church by going door-to-door as an evangelist for many years," Matthew said. "He also told me that very few missionaries go that deep into the rural countryside and that many of them will not travel past Eldoret. He also said it would be a great honor to have an American evangelist preach in his church."

"How long will it take to get there?" Michelle asked.

"If we took public transportation from Nairobi to Kisumu, it would be a very long and painful ordeal; so a better option would be to book a forty-minute flight on Kenya Airways," Matthew said. "Once we arrive in Kisumu, Pastor Thompson will meet us at the airport."

"What would we be doing once we get there?" Michelle asked.

"We could spend several weeks ministering in Pastor Thompson's church," Matthew said. "When I searched the satellite images on the Internet, there are very few paved roads in his area. It's mostly rural countryside and farming villages surrounded by lush rolling hills. If we traveled northwest from Kisumu, we could visit Uganda. If we traveled west, we would run into Lake Victoria. It's also close to the Tanzania border, but we would have to travel through Maasai territory to get there."

"Is it safe to travel through Maasai territory?" Michelle asked.

"The Maasai consider themselves to be a warrior tribe," Matthew said. "They like dressing up in red garments. They also specialize in cattle ranching and own large tracts of land near the Tanzania border. If we crossed into Tanzania, we could visit the Serengeti Plain. The entire region is where everybody likes going on safari because it's home to the Mara Triangle and the Masai Mara National Reserve."

"That sounds like an incredible adventure," Michelle said. "When do you want to leave?"

* * *

When Draven discovered the missionaries' plans to minister in Pastor Thompson's church, he left Dragon-Claw's territory and began searching the rural countryside to find out what techniques the local principalities were using to ensnare souls in the area.

* * *

After the missionaries made all the necessary travel arrangements to leave Nairobi, they boarded a flight to Kisumu. When they arrived at the airport in Kisumu, Matthew located a ticket counter and negotiated a price for public transportation so they could travel to Kisii Town. When they met Pastor Thompson at a restaurant in Kisii Town, he said, "I am so happy you are here."

"It's so beautiful in this part of Kenya," Michelle said. "I love the rural countryside, the scenic hilltop views and even the farm animals that were walking down the center of the road."

"We have been ministering in Kibera, and it feels so good to get away from that dark, dirty, polluted and hostile environment," Matthew said.

"You are most welcome here," Pastor Thompson said. "Are you staying in Kisii Town?"

"We don't have a place yet," Michelle said.

"You are welcome to stay at my house," Pastor

Thompson said. "My wife will prepare a room for you."

"How far away do you live from Kisii Town?" Michelle asked.

"I live near the Nyamasege Junction," Pastor Thompson said. "It takes a little over an hour to reach my house when the roads are dry."

"We wanted to stay at a location that's close to a major grocery store," Michelle said. "Matthew made me promise that we wouldn't eat any food in Kenya that we didn't prepare ourselves."

"I understand your concerns," Pastor Thompson said. "Instead of staying at my house, a better option would be at the Hilltop Hotel. It's located near the Ogembo Junction. There's an outdoor market at the junction that sells fresh fruit, vegetables, beans, rice and potatoes—everything you will need.

"There's even a general store at the junction that sells bread, cleaning supplies and bottled water. The cost to rent a room has increased. The hotel recently raised prices to a thousand shillings per night, but they operate a gas-powered generator that will provide electricity."

"Do you think they will give us a discount if we rent two rooms for two weeks?" Matthew asked.

"I would be happy to negotiate a lower price for you with the hotel manager," Pastor Thompson said.

* * *

After the missionaries got settled into their rooms at the Hilltop Hotel, they made plans to minister at Pastor Thompson's church on Sunday. When Sunday morning arrived, Pastor Thompson picked up the missionaries in front of the hotel and said, "My church members are very happy that you are coming today. My wife wanted to prepare a meal for you, but I told her that you will not require any food, upon your own request."

"Thank you for your hospitality and your understanding," Michelle said. "It means a lot to us."

Pastor Thompson's church had been built on an elevated section of land near his house. When the missionaries arrived, they had to jump across a ravine to reach a set of stairs that looked more like a ladder that had been embedded into the dirt. After climbing the ladder to reach the top landing, the missionaries followed Pastor Thompson past a large wooden structure that was being used as his church.

After passing the church that was starting to fill with people, the missionaries walked by the outdoor restroom facilities before climbing another set of stairs. When they reached the top landing, they passed by two cows that were tied up next to a feeding trough, a small chicken coop, and a wooden hut that his wife used as a kitchen. A small garden had been planted next to Pastor Thompson's house, and when they walked through the doorway, Pastor Thompson said, "This is my wife, Tabatha."

"It's very good to meet you," Michelle said. "You have such a lovely home."

"Thank you," Tabatha said. "My husband and I built it ourselves many years ago."

"I noticed a solar panel on your roof," Matthew said. "I have never seen anything like that before. How does it work?"

"The solar panel charges a car battery during the day," Pastor Thompson said. "Then at night, we use the car battery to operate a twelve-volt light bulb that we have attached to the ceiling."

"Do you have an inverter that can convert twelve volt electricity from a car battery into one hundred and twenty volt electricity?" Matthew asked.

"We don't have an inverter, but we have a gas-powered generator that we use to operate the sound equipment in the church," Pastor Thompson said.

"Where do you get your water?" Matthew asked.

"During the rainy season, we collect water from the roof," Pastor Thompson said. "It drains through a series of gutters and downspouts, and then we collect it into plastic barrels around the house. During the dry season, my wife and children fetch water from the stream that flows in the valley about five hundred meters behind my house."

"In America, we would call this off-grid living," Matthew said. "It's a very popular trend where people are moving out of the big cities to get away from all the crime and pollution. A lot of families just want to be self-reliant and live a simpler life by growing their own food, drinking clean water and being less dependent on the electrical grid."

"Do you cook your meals over an open fire?" Michelle asked.

"The smoke inside the kitchen causes a lot of women in Kenya to experience asthma and other difficulties breathing," Tabatha said. "That is why we are trusting in the Lord to provide us with a gas cooker."

When Pastor Thompson heard the sound of music coming from his church, he said, "The service is about to begin. We have prepared a special place for you in front of the congregation."

When the missionaries entered the large wooden structure, there were several rows of children sitting in the front, followed by a center section that was filled with women who were all wearing brightly colored clothing.

Most of the young men were standing in the back, while the older men were seated in chairs. When it came time for Matthew to deliver his message, he stood in front of the audience next to Pastor Thompson, who wanted to translate the message into the Kisii language.

Matthew began by saying, "Please turn with me to the Gospel of John." Because everybody in the church remained motionless, Matthew asked the audience, "How many people own their own Bible?"

After looking around, there were only three people in the back section who raised their hands. When Matthew turned around to look at the elders who were seated in the front, there were only two people who raised their hands.

"I would like to help you fix that problem," Matthew said. "I think everybody in this church needs their own Bible, so I'm going to work with Pastor Thompson to figure out a way to buy some Bibles in the Kisii language."

After Pastor Thompson translated that statement into the Kisii language, everybody in the audience erupted with a joy-filled expression of excitement.

"I'm going to read all the Scripture passages for today's sermon very slowly," Matthew said. "I want everybody to pay special attention, because at the end of the message, I'm going to ask you some questions about the Old Testament. The person who provides the correct answer is going to receive a free Kisii Bible.

"So let's begin with the Gospel of John. In chapter one, God's Word says, 'In the beginning was the Word, and the Word was with God, and the Word was God. He was in the beginning with God. All things came into being through him, and without him not one thing came into being.'[46] From this Scripture passage, we know that Jesus existed before the beginning of time.

"If Jesus existed before the beginning of time, it would make sense that there would be some Scripture passages written about him before he was born. Before we look at some Old Testament examples that point toward Jesus, let's study a passage of Scripture from the Gospel of Luke. In the twenty-fourth chapter, two disciples were traveling on the road to Emmaus. As they were walking along, Jesus approached these men and began walking beside them. Because they were unable to recognize him, Jesus said to them, 'What are you discussing with each other while you walk along?'[47]

"One of the disciples responded by saying, 'Are you the only stranger in Jerusalem who does not know the things that have taken place there in these days?'[48] When Jesus asked the disciples to explain what happened, they described how the chief priests and leaders handed him over to be crucified.

"Then in verse twenty-five, Jesus said to these men, '"Oh, how foolish you are, and how slow of heart to believe all that the prophets have declared! Was it not necessary that the Messiah should suffer these things and then enter into his glory?" Then beginning with Moses and all the prophets, he interpreted to them the things about himself in all the Scriptures.'[49]

"Can you imagine what it would be like to be walking alongside the disciples and hear what Jesus had to say? Jesus said it was necessary for the Messiah to suffer a painful death on the cross so that he could pay the penalty for our sins, and then he interpreted for them all the things written about him in the Scriptures. Then in verse forty-four Jesus says, '"These are my words that I spoke to you while I was still with you—that everything written about me in the law of Moses, the prophets, and the psalms must be fulfilled." Then he opened their minds to understand the Scriptures.'[50]

"My question for you today is: What things were written about Jesus in the Old Testament? Can anyone give me an example?"

Because the entire audience remained silent, Matthew removed several sheets of paper from his notebook and said, "I have a list of over two hundred Bible prophecies from the Old Testament that Jesus needed to fulfill in the New Testament. I'm going to give this list to Pastor Thompson in case he wants to preach a sermon series on these passages.

"Let me share with you one of my favorite passages from the Prophet Isaiah, who said, 'He was wounded for our transgressions, crushed for our iniquities; upon him was the punishment that made us whole, and by his bruises we are healed. Like a lamb that is led to the slaughter, and like a sheep that before its shearers is silent, so he did not open his mouth. They made his grave with the wicked and his tomb with the rich, although he had done no violence, and there was no deceit in his mouth.'[51]

"This passage of Scripture from the Book of Isaiah was written seven hundred years before Jesus was born, and it describes the kind of death the Messiah would need to suffer. Jesus was able to fulfill this passage of Scripture from the Old Testament when he died on the cross for the forgiveness of our sins.

"Another example that was written hundreds of years before Jesus was born comes from the Book of Psalms that says, 'My God, my God, why have you forsaken me?'[52] Then in verses sixteen and eighteen, 'For dogs are all around me; a company of evildoers encircles me. They divide my clothes among themselves, and for my clothing they cast lots.'[53]

"I'm sure everybody knows how these prophecies of Scripture were fulfilled hundreds of years later when Jesus was crucified on the cross of Calvary for the forgiveness of our sins; so let me give you a few more examples from the New Testament, and then you tell me a corresponding event from the Old Testament.

"In the Gospel of John, when John the Baptist saw Jesus approaching, he said, 'Here is the Lamb of God who takes away the sin of the world!'[54] There was also a lamb in the Old Testament that allowed the angel of death to pass over a person's house. God gave special instructions in the Book of Exodus that none of the lamb's bones shall be broken.[55] What is the corresponding event in the Old Testament?"

"The Jewish Passover," one man said, who was standing in the back of the church.

"Congratulations, you just won the first Bible," Matthew said. "Another opportunity for the second Bible comes from the Gospel of John where Jesus says, 'I am the bread of life.'[56] He also said, 'I am the living bread that came down from heaven.'[57] Can anyone give me an example from the Old Testament where God fed his children with bread that came down from heaven?"[58]

"Manna in the wilderness," a woman said who was seated in the center section.

"Very good," Matthew said. "In some translations of the Bible, Jesus describes himself as a door for the sheep. In the Gospel of John, Jesus says, 'I am the gate. Whoever enters by me will be saved.'[59] In a similar way, there was a door in the Old Testament that everybody needed to enter before they could be saved.[60] Can anyone think of a doorway where all the people and all the animals needed to enter before they could be saved?"

"Noah's Ark," another woman said.

"The next example may be more challenging," Matthew said. "When Jesus was speaking with Nathanael, he said, 'You will see heaven opened and the angels of God ascending and descending upon the Son of Man.'[61] Can anyone give me an example from the Old Testament when the angels of God were ascending and descending between heaven and earth?"

Because nobody in the audience could answer the question Matthew said, "Because Jesus is our connection between heaven and earth, that connection would also serve as a bridge. There was also a corresponding connection or bridge in the Old Testament that resembled a stairway."[62]

"The vision of Jacob's ladder," a young man said.

After Matthew shared many other examples from the Old Testament describing how Jesus needed to suffer an agonizing death on the cross to pay the penalty for our sins, he concluded his message with a prayer of repentance. During the prayer, he challenged the audience to surrender their lives to Jesus, so they could be filled with the Holy Spirit and accomplish the Father's will in their lives.

9th CHAPTER

After the service ended, when Michelle was handing out vanilla toffees to the children, Pastor Thompson approached Matthew and said, "Everybody was so greatly encouraged by your message. We are so thankful for your offer to provide us with some Kisii Bibles."

"Do they sell Kisii Bibles around here?" Matthew asked.

"The local dealers are asking one thousand shillings for a hard-cover edition," Pastor Thompson said. "That's why nobody in my church can afford one."

"Where do the local dealers get their Bibles?" Matthew asked.

"They come from the Kenya Bible Society in Nairobi," the Pastor said.

"I'm wondering if we could get a better discount if we placed a large order directly through the Bible Society," Matthew said.

"That would be such a blessing for my church," Pastor Thompson said.

"Would you like to meet with us tomorrow morning to discuss plans for a community outreach?" Matthew asked. "We could meet you at a restaurant or stop by your house. Another option would be to meet at our hotel, and we will make you some African flatbread for breakfast."

"I can stop by your hotel around ten o'clock in the morning," Pastor Thompson said. "After I take care of my farm animals, I have an early morning appointment, so it will work out well with my schedule."

* * *

The following morning, when Pastor Thompson arrived at the missionaries' hotel, Michelle greeted him at the door and said, "Please come in. I have been cooking flatbread all morning."

"It smells delicious," the Pastor said.

"The religious sisters in Nairobi showed me how to make them," Michelle said.

"Your wife mentioned that she wanted a gas cooker the other day," Matthew said. "I think we need to get one ourselves. Since the electricity only comes on at night, we're not able to use our electric hotplate during the day. I have been using our camping stove, but it's running out of fuel, and I don't think we are going to be able to buy another cylinder around here."

"Do you know where we can buy a gas cooker?" Michelle asked.

"They sell them in Kisii Town," Pastor Thompson said. "Some models have one burner, but others have two or three burners. They also sell pressure regulators, rubber hoses and propane tanks."

"Maybe we could take your wife shopping for a gas cooker sometime this week," Michelle said.

"She would like that," Pastor Thompson said.

"Do you have any ideas for a community outreach?" Matthew asked.

"There are many non-believers who don't practice any kind of religion in this area," the Pastor said. "It will not be easy to reach them, because the roads are extremely rough, and they become impassable during the rainy season."

"Why can't we use the roads when it rains?" Michelle asked.

"The tarmac roads are always open," Pastor Thompson said. "During the rainy season, when it rains all month, there is so much mud that even large tractors have a difficult time. In a passenger vehicle, the tire treads will fill with mud, causing the wheels to spin until the road dries out. If we get trapped in a heavy rainstorm, we would have to spend the night in the car or leave the car behind and hire motorbikes to bring us back home."

"If we wanted to conduct an outreach in a remote area, how would you gather the people for a community meeting?" Matthew asked.

"The first step would be to inform the village chief," Pastor Thompson said. "We would give him a place of honor at the meeting and allow him some time to address the community's concerns with any public service announcements that he wanted to make."

"Do you think the village chief would help us advertise the meeting by passing out flyers to all the residents?" Michelle asked.

"Once the village chief approves the day and time for the meeting, we could give him the flyers for distribution," Pastor Thompson said. "We could also distribute the flyers in the town square. Another option would be to distribute the flyers along with a personal invitation by going door-to-door to people's homes."

"Is it possible to set up sound equipment in a remote area with a gas-powered generator?" Matthew asked.

"I know a man who has an amplifier that runs off a car battery," Pastor Thompson said. "We could use the generator and sound equipment from my church, but the speakers are very large and too heavy to transport. I wouldn't want the equipment to get ruined during a rainstorm, so a better option would be to rent a portable unit."

"Are there any Muslims in the area?" Matthew asked.

"There are very few Muslims around here," Pastor Thompson said. "By God's grace, Islam hasn't taken root in this part of Kenya."

"What do you think we should call the community outreach meeting?" Matthew asked.

"I think we should call it a Fellowship Meeting

based on God's Word," Michelle said. "How about, 'Come and experience the transforming power of God's Word! This two-hour Fellowship Meeting begins at nine o'clock and concludes at eleven o'clock.'"

"I like the idea of a fellowship meeting," Pastor Thompson said. "I know of many rural villages that don't have any churches in the area. It would be very easy to gather all the believers and non-believers together in an attempt to establish a new church."

After the missionaries finalized plans for an outreach, Matthew took out five thousand shillings from his travel wallet and said to the Pastor, "I hope this is enough money to cover the cost of your transportation so that you can start visiting the village chiefs."

"Thank you very much," Pastor Thompson said. "You are very generous. I will start contacting the village chiefs tomorrow."

"I have a request that's very important," Michelle said. "When you are scheduling the outreach meetings with the village chiefs, please make sure the dates don't conflict with any other events in the area. If the community market days are held on Wednesday and Saturday, and if everyone is busy buying and selling goods on those days, then nobody will come to our meeting."

"I understand your concern," the Pastor said. "I will inquire about the market days and other events before I finalize the outreach meetings with the chiefs."

* * *

When Draven discovered the missionaries' plans

to conduct outreach meetings in the area, he softened his shadow-stalking appearance and made his presence known to the leader of the demonic principality that was using the Ogembo Police Department for his base of operations.

When Draven entered into Bloodhoof's presence, he said, "I need your help to exterminate two missionaries who are planning to build a church in your area."

"I am aware of their presence," Bloodhoof said. "I will assign my best destroyer to help you. He specializes in causing automobile accidents. When the monkeys get drunk, he's very good at distracting them so they crash into each other. I like watching the excitement when they start fighting with each other after the collision."

"Where can I find the destroyer?" Draven asked.

"His name is Thrall and he's working a section of highway near the sugarcane factory," Bloodhoof said.

"I will keep you informed," Draven said as he departed into the night sky.

* * *

The next day when Pastor Thompson stopped by the missionaries' hotel, he said, "I met with three village chiefs yesterday afternoon, and they were all very happy that we wanted to conduct a community meeting in their district. I set up the first meeting for next week on Friday morning at nine o'clock. The other two meetings were scheduled the following week on Tuesday and Thursday at ten o'clock in the morning."

"I already have the basic design for the flyers,"

Michelle said. "Now that we know the dates and times, all I need is a description of the meeting location. Are we going to meet under a shade tree on someone's property, or are we meeting in the town square?"

"I still need to work out those details with the local landowners," the Pastor said.

"I was able to buy a hundred Kisii Bibles and thirty Swahili Bibles from the Kenya Bible Society," Matthew said. "I spent a long time negotiating with the sales department, and the best price they would give me was eight hundred and fifty shillings per Bible."

"That's a very good price," Pastor Thompson said.

"It's still a lot of money in American dollars, so we need to be very careful on how we give them away," Matthew said.

* * *

When Draven approached the section of the highway near the sugarcane factory, he found Thrall hovering over a group of motorcycle taxi drivers who had been drinking. After observing how the destroyer was influencing the men's thoughts, he waited until Thrall was finished, then approached him with their new assignment by saying, "Bloodhoof wants us to work together to exterminate two American missionaries who are planning to build a church in the area."

"That should be easy," Thrall said.

"The missionaries have an elite team of guardian angels who are constantly watching over them," Draven said. "We have not been able to tempt them into committing any deadly sins, and they are constantly praying."

"We have a network of witch doctors who cast spells on pastors in the area," Thrall said. "If you show me where the monkeys are planning to build a church, I'm sure we can eliminate them before they get started."

* * *

After the missionaries made all the necessary preparations, they arrived early Friday morning to set up the sound equipment near a large rock outcrop. All the residents who lived in that area knew about the location, because there was a small stream that flowed over the face of the cliff that created a misty waterfall.

The farmers who lived in the nearby adobe houses had already started to congregate in a grassy area about one hundred meters away from the main road. After Pastor Thompson finished setting up the sound equipment, the village chief arrived in a truck that was filled with plastic chairs. Not long after, Pastor Thompson began the meeting by introducing his guests, then he turned the meeting over to the chief who addressed several community-related issues with the residents.

When it came time for Matthew to deliver his message, he held up a Kisii Bible and said, "I would like to share with you the power of God's Word that's contained in this book. This is no ordinary book. This book is thousands of years old. It's the best-selling book in the world, and it comes in the Kisii language.

"Many people call this book *God's Word* because

it contains the story of salvation; and the information contained in this book applies to every person in the entire world. The story of salvation begins in the chapter of Genesis when God created Adam and Eve for fellowship. God loved Adam and Eve very much, and he used to walk with them, hand-in-hand, during the time of the evening breeze.[63]

"Then something very bad happened. In the back of this book, there's a chapter called Revelation that gives us more information. Because God loved Adam and Eve so much, some of the angels became very jealous. They didn't think humans deserved to be loved so much by God, so the highest-ranking angel, named Lucifer, staged a rebellion. After Lucifer persuaded a third of the heavenly host to join him in the rebellion, a great war broke out in heaven.[64]

"The Book of Revelation says that 'Michael and his angels fought against the dragon. The dragon and his angels fought back, but they were defeated, and there was no longer any place for them in heaven. The great dragon was thrown down, that ancient serpent, who is called the Devil and Satan, the deceiver of the whole world—he was thrown down to the earth, and his angels were thrown down with him.'[65]

"After Lucifer and all the fallen angels lost the battle, they were stripped of their power and cast out of heaven. Because there wasn't any place for the fallen angels to go, they descended upon the earth in great wrath. It was Lucifer's plan to attack Adam and Eve and trick them into committing the first sin. Lucifer knew that if Adam and Eve committed a sin, that sin would create a barrier that would separate God from his beloved creation; that's because God is perfectly holy, and nothing evil can enter into his presence.

"After Adam and Eve committed the first sin by eating from the tree in the center of the garden, a separation occurred. God could no longer interact with his beloved children the same as before. Because God still loved Adam and Eve very much, he didn't give up on humanity; instead, he set up a system of religious rules and regulations that are described in the first five books of the Bible. You can read about this system of religious practices that are described in the books of Genesis, Exodus, Leviticus, Numbers and Deuteronomy.

"God also gave us the Ten Commandments and declared the penalty for sin to be death. When one of Adam and Eve's descendants committed a sin, a penalty needed to be paid. Because the penalty for sin was death, God allowed the death penalty to be placed upon an innocent lamb. The lamb was slaughtered in the temple and the blood of the lamb atoned for the man's sin. The man was allowed to live, and the lamb paid the death penalty on the man's behalf.

"This system worked great for hundreds of years. The only problem was that people just kept sinning and sacrificing. Because everybody was sinning and sacrificing innocent lambs in the temple, God sent many prophets to declare a New Covenant. You can read the words of these prophets in the center of the Bible in the chapters known as Isaiah, Jeremiah and Ezekiel.

"Let me give you an example from the prophet Jeremiah who said, 'The days are surely coming, says the Lord, when I will make a new covenant with the house of Israel and the house of Judah. It will not be like the covenant that I made with their ancestors when I took them by the hand to bring them out of the land of Egypt—a covenant that they broke, though I was their husband, says the Lord. But this is the covenant that I will make with the house of Israel after those days, says the Lord: I will put my law within them, and I will write it on their hearts; and I will be their God, and they shall be my people.'[66]

"After God sent many prophets into the world to declare the Old Covenant was about to expire and that a New Covenant was coming, he sent his only begotten Son into the world to take the place of the sacrificial lamb. After the long-awaited Messiah was born, we started celebrating his birth at Christmas, which makes me wonder: How many people celebrate Christmas?"

Because half the people in the audience raised their hands, Matthew continued by saying, "At Christmas, we celebrate the birth of Christ. God sent an angel named Gabriel to a virgin named Mary who lived in the town of Nazareth. The angel said to her, 'Do not be afraid, Mary, for you have found favor with God. And now, you will conceive in your womb and bear a son, and you will name him Jesus.'[67]

"Then Mary said to the angel, 'How can this be, since I am a virgin?'[68]

"The angel said to Mary, 'The Holy Spirit will come upon you, and the power of the Most High will overshadow you; therefore the child to be born will be holy; he will be called Son of God.'[69]

"Because Jesus experienced a supernatural birth through the power of the Holy Spirit, he is both fully divine and fully human. One of Jesus' names is Emmanuel, which means, 'God is with us.'[70] Because Jesus is the divine manifestation of God's Spirit in human form, he was able to live a supernatural life. Jesus was able to walk on water and feed a multitude of people with five loaves of bread and two fish.[71] He healed the sick, cleansed the lepers and raised the dead to life.[72] You can read about all of the miracles that Jesus performed in the Gospels of Matthew, Mark, Luke and John.

"Then in the fullness of time, Jesus took the place of the sacrificial lamb. He was arrested, tortured and crucified. After dying on the cross for the forgiveness of our sins, they buried him in a tomb; and on the third day, he rose from the dead. After Jesus rose from the dead, he appeared to his disciples and promised to send the Holy Spirit.[73] Once his disciples received power from the Holy Spirit on the Day of Pentecost, they went forth to transform the world. You can read about how the disciples healed the sick, cast out demons, proclaimed the Good News and established churches in the Book of Acts, along with the other letters in the back of this book.

"I wanted to share with you a summary of salvation history that's contained in the Bible, because the message of salvation applies to everyone who is present in the audience today. Although this book is thousands of years old, it applies to everyone because the penalty for sin is still death. Because everyone present today is a sinner, we all have a choice to make: We can pay the death penalty ourselves, or we can allow Jesus to pay the death penalty on our behalf.

"Does anyone in the audience want to pay the death penalty themselves? Please raise your hand if you want to pay the death penalty for your own sins."

Because nobody in the audience raised their hands, Matthew said, "Please raise your hand if you want Jesus to pay the death penalty on your behalf."

Because everybody in the audience raised their hands, Matthew said, "I would like to lead you in a prayer for salvation, but the problem is, I can't pray this prayer on your behalf. You will need to pray this prayer yourselves because this prayer is between your heart and God. So let's take a moment of silence to examine our hearts and get ready to pray."

After leading the audience in a prayer for salvation, Matthew said, "I'm looking for ten volunteers who are leaders in the community. I would like five men and five women to please come forward."

Because the majority of the people in the audience were hesitant, Matthew started pointing at people in the audience whom he felt a spiritual connection with while he was preaching. After selecting five men and five women, he asked the volunteers to stand in front of the gathering while Pastor Thompson brought over a box of Bibles.

After Matthew gave every volunteer a Bible, he said, "I would like for you to set up a fellowship group in your homes so that you can share God's Word with your friends and neighbors. Is everybody willing to do that?"

After all the volunteers agreed, Pastor Thompson said, "Let us pray over our Bible study leaders so they may receive an abundant outpouring of the Holy Spirit's power to carry out their assignments."

After praying over the volunteers, Pastor Thompson asked the village chief to come forward to receive a present. Matthew presented the first gift by handing him a Swahili Bible, and then Michelle presented the chief with an assortment of chocolate candies that had been wrapped in white construction paper and decorated with a red ribbon that she had formed into a bow.

After Pastor Thompson asked the audience to express their appreciation to the village chief for setting up the meeting, the farmers returned to their homes.

10th CHAPTER

While the missionaries were driving back home, Michelle asked, "Is there a place we can pull over to discuss the outreach?"

"What's wrong?" Matthew asked.

"This road is way too rough to talk about it inside the car," Michelle said. "We're bouncing around all over the place, and there's a nice scenic overview along this section of the road."

After the driver stopped the car, Pastor Thompson and the missionaries walked down the embankment about thirty meters and took seats on a rock outcrop overlooking the farmland below. After a long moment of silence Michelle said, "That was the perfect place to build a church. We had over a hundred people in attendance, enough for a Christian community, and it feels like we just abandoned the entire congregation."

"What do you mean?" Matthew asked. "I thought it was an excellent outreach. I wish we had more money to give every person in the audience a Bible, but because we don't, I chose ten leaders who agreed to start study groups in their homes."

"We don't even know if those people can read," Michelle said. "Even if they can read, they are going to need help understanding the Scriptures before they can apply God's Word to their lives. It's also very unlikely that any of the newly formed Bible study groups will be able to work together with the other groups in the area to build a church by themselves."

"What do you suggest?" Matthew asked.

"It's mostly my fault," Michelle said. "I should have been interacting with our guests in an attempt to get everybody's names and cell phone numbers. I could feel the Holy Spirit prompting me to make a guest list, but I was hesitant because they don't have any electricity, computers, email accounts or a cyber cafe in the area. I'm not even sure if they have a mailing address, a street number or a mailbox in front of their homes, much less any other way of contacting them except for knocking on their front doors."

"I was able to build my church by going door-to-door as an evangelist," Pastor Thompson said. "After gathering a small community of believers, we started meeting underneath an acacia tree. Within a year, we were able to build a shade canopy that we used for our community meetings. After the shade canopy was destroyed by a flood, I traded a piece of farmland for the property behind my house so that my wife and I could build our church."

"How much does it cost to buy a piece of land big enough to build a church?" Matthew asked.

"It depends on the location," Pastor Thompson said. "Land that has access to a road will cost more than land without vehicle access. If you wanted to buy a piece of property near the waterfall outreach location, it would probably cost one hundred thousand shillings."

"How much is that in American dollars?" Michelle asked,

"It's about a thousand dollars," Matthew said.

"If you wanted to build a large church with a corrugated tin roof, outdoor restroom facilities and a small office for the pastor, it would cost an additional hundred thousand shillings," Pastor Thompson said. "The sound equipment and bench seating would cost another fifty thousand shillings."

"Are you thinking we should build a church back there?" Matthew asked.

"It was an incredibly beautiful location with a flowing stream and a waterfall," Michelle said. "It was located in the center of the community for easy access. The property was close enough to the main road so that the church members could build a sign to advertise their service times."

"From my experience, it requires more than three hundred thousand shillings to build a successful church," Pastor Thompson said. "The first requirement is God's presence. You will need the power and presence of God in your church so that the Holy Spirit can do his work in the minds and hearts of your church members. You will also need a dedicated community of believers who want to grow in holiness. You will need people who are hungry for God's presence—a community of believers who want to surrender their hearts to the Lord—so they can accomplish God's will in their lives.

"Another important requirement for a successful church is the building. Many churches in Africa have been started underneath a shade tree, but because of the heavy rains in Kenya, it will be necessary to build a structure as soon as possible. Having a roof over their heads will not only give your church members a place they can call home, but it will also let your congregation know that you are serious in providing for both their spiritual and physical needs."

"It sounds like a lot of work," Matthew said.

"Let me give you an example of a church that has been built with a lot of money but is devoid of God's presence," Pastor Thompson said. "In the Maasai lands, there was a rich man who donated a lot of money to build a church. It was the nicest structure that I have ever seen in this area.

"The Maasai pastor wanted to build a church so large that it needed custom-built trusses made out of metal. They used concrete cinder blocks to build the exterior walls and covered them with stucco. The rich man even paid a lot of money to buy a very expensive sound system.

"Because this church was so big, the pastor could

never fill the worship area with people, so it always had a half-empty feeling. Instead of spending time in God's presence, reading God's Word so that the church leadership could deliver a powerful message on Sunday, the pastor allowed his church members to share their personal testimonies and praise reports for the majority of the service.

"Although this approach may have helped the members of his congregation feel more connected to the community, it didn't take long before one church member said something that another church member didn't like. Soon, conflicts started to arise within his community regarding who would receive the most microphone time. If the pastor favored the rich members over the poorest church members who didn't give as much money, it would be easy to understand why his congregation continues to struggle to this very day."

"That's a good example of why we should use our limited time and resources on evangelization," Matthew said.

"Let me share a passage of Scripture with you that may shed more light on this situation from a different perspective," Pastor Thompson said. "The passage is from the Gospel of Luke in the seventeenth chapter where Jesus says, 'Who among you would say to your slave who has just come in from plowing or tending sheep in the field, "Come here at once and take your place at the table"?'[74]

"'Would you not rather say to him, "Prepare supper

for me, put on your apron and serve me while I eat and drink; later you may eat and drink"? Do you thank the slave for doing what was commanded? So you also, when you have done all that you were ordered to do, say, "We are worthless slaves; we have done only what we ought to have done!"'[75]

"In this passage, there are two types of servants. One servant works hard all day plowing the field. This man represents the evangelist who goes around sowing seeds on good soil in an attempt to produce a rich harvest for God's kingdom.[76] The other servant works hard all day long tending the flock. This man represents the pastor who spends his time caring for the sheep.[77]

"After both servants work hard all day plowing rocky soil and tending a rebellious flock of stubborn goats, we are both required to put on our aprons, enter into the Lord's presence, and minister to the Lord through our praise and worship. At the end of the passage, Jesus says to both men: If you only did what was commanded of you, then consider yourself a worthless servant.

"Because I would never want to be called a worthless servant by my Lord and Master, I am going to go well beyond the call of duty. If the Lord is calling me to do the work of the pastor, tending his flock day and night so that not one is lost or missing, then I will also do the work of the evangelist by helping you plow the hard ground, so that together, we may produce a rich harvest for the Lord. That way, we will both have the opportunity to hear our Master say, 'Well done, good and trustworthy slave.'"[78]

"In addition to that Scripture passage, the Great Commission calls us to make disciples of all nations," Michelle said.[79] "There's a difference between making disciples out of those men and women back there and just giving them a Bible and telling them to set up their own Bible study groups. Instead of sending them back to their homes so they can make disciples out of themselves, we need to go back there and help them."

"I can send some of my church elders to help with the Bible study groups," Pastor Thompson said. "I have spent a lot of time making disciples out of the men and women in my church, and it's about time they go out into the community to teach others what they have learned."

* * *

Early Tuesday morning, when Pastor Thompson stopped by the missionaries' hotel to pick them up for the next outreach meeting, he said, "The village chief was very helpful at setting up the community meeting. We are expecting around one hundred and fifty people, but instead of meeting in the town square, the chief moved the meeting to a vacant lot that's located next to the primary school."

As the missionaries were approaching the outreach location, Michelle looked out the car window and said, "Look at those zebras over there that are grazing behind that huge pile of bricks."

"The people who live in this community make bricks as their professional trade," Pastor Thompson said. "They store them in mounds alongside the road until they can find a buyer."

"Do you think they would give us a ministry discount if we wanted to buy a lot of bricks to build a church?" Michelle asked.

"You will also need to buy cement and hire the masons," Pastor Thompson said as the driver parked in front of the vacant lot that was located next to the school.

After Pastor Thompson set up the portable sound equipment, he began the meeting in prayer and then invited the village chief to come forward to address the audience with all of his community-related concerns. After the village chief made all of his public service announcements, Pastor Thompson introduced his guests from America to the audience.

When it came time for Matthew to deliver his message, he started his sermon by introducing the Kisii Bible to the audience. He delivered the same message as before, except at the end of the sermon, after everybody had accepted the Gospel message, he asked the audience a simple question: "Are there any churches in the area?"

Because the majority of the people in the audience remained silent, with only a few people saying, "No," Matthew said, "I'm wondering if there's anyone in the audience who would be willing to donate a small piece of land so that we could build a church.

"A church is more than a building where we could meet together to worship God. A church is even more than a place where we can experience the power and presence of God together. A church is a community of believers who love and support each other.[80] For example, if there was a woman from this community who was hurting and in need of help, the other women in the church could surround her and embrace her with loving arms. They could support her, encourage her and pray with her. They could even combine their resources together to help her through a difficult situation.

"The same concept also applies to the men in this community. Because men have the ability to inspire and encourage each other, in the same way that iron sharpens iron, the men in this community have the ability to help other men become more powerful leaders.

"Another reason why you are going to want to form a church is for your own personal protection. I have already shared with you how Satan and a third of the fallen angels were cast out of heaven. Those demonic forces haven't gone anywhere. They are still down here trying to harm as many people as possible. According to the Bible, Satan only has one purpose—to steal, kill and destroy.[81]

"Knowing that we have a deadly enemy who wants to separate us from God's blessings, I think every man here would want to know how to protect himself and his family from the devil's deadly attacks. Because the only way to protect yourself is by entering into an authentic relationship with Jesus, striving for holiness and putting on the full armor of God as described in Saint Paul's letter to the Ephesians, I think every man in attendance today would want to sign up for our weekly Bible study group to learn more information.

"If you want to be part of a loving Christian community that supports and encourages each other, please give Michelle your contact information. We will need to know how to contact you so that we can start meeting together. I would like to set up several weekly Bible study groups so that we can build a church together."

* * *

When Draven saw the effect that Matthew was having on the audience, he said, "The big monkey does this everywhere he goes. We haven't been able to stop him."

"Let's influence some troublemakers to attend the next meeting," Thrall said. "All we need is a drunkard who will start causing problems so we can destroy the fellowship using their own members."

* * *

After the service, Michelle found herself surrounded by a large group of people who wanted to sign up for the weekly Bible study group. She was able to fill seven notebook pages with the names, occupations and occasionally a few cell phone numbers of everyone interested in meeting on Saturday afternoon.

After Matthew finished helping Pastor Thompson load the sound equipment in the back of the car, he approached Michelle and said, "Do you want to walk over to the school to see if it's possible to rent a classroom for the Saturday afternoon Bible study group?"

"The Principal of the school attended our meeting," Michelle said, flipping through the pages of her notebook to find his contact information. "His name is Patterson Onyango, and I have his cell number."

"Let's bring him one of the Swahili Bibles as a present," Pastor Thompson said.

When the Pastor and the missionaries entered the school property through the main gate, they walked past several classrooms that were filled with different age groups of children who were all wearing similar uniforms. The majority of the boys were wearing white shirts and blue pants, while the girls wore white blouses, blue skirts and shiny black shoes. After entering the school office, the missionaries were greeted by a friendly receptionist who invited them into Principal Patterson's office.

"You are most welcome here," the Principal said, walking over to shake everyone's hand.

"It's a beautiful school you have here," Michelle said.

"We wanted to give you a Swahili Bible as a present," Matthew said. "We also wanted to inquire about the possibility of renting several classrooms on Saturday afternoon to conduct a community Bible study meeting."

"That would be most wonderful," the Principal said. "You are welcome to use our facilities during the weekends. I only ask that you help us by providing some school supplies for our children."

"What kind do you need?" Michelle asked.

"Mostly paper and pencils," the Principal said.

"We would be happy to supply your school with as much paper and pencils as you need," Matthew said. "I don't think they have any office supply stores around here, but the next time we are in Kisii Town, we will buy everything we can find."

"My students and teachers would be most grateful," Principal Patterson said.

"I will also ask my mother to send us a box of school supplies," Michelle said. "In America, we have discount stores where it's possible to buy items for one dollar. They sell scissors, calculators, crayons, paper clips, tape and colored highlighting markers, all for a dollar. It would even be possible to buy several packages of those tiny pencil sharpeners so that your students could sharpen their own pencils."

"That would be such a blessing," the Principal said. "I am also looking forward to learning more about the power of God's Word in your Bible study classes. The graduate-level education that you can provide to our community will be invaluable."

After the missionaries arranged a time to meet Principal Patterson on Saturday afternoon, they thanked him for his hospitality. As they were walking back to the vehicle, Michelle said, "I'm still worried about the waterfall location. Can we stop by there on the way home? I wanted to go door-to-door to check on the progress of our Bible study groups."

"I would also like to stop by the schools in that area to see if we can rent more classrooms," Pastor Thompson said.

* * *

Several hours before the Thursday morning outreach was scheduled to begin, Pastor Thompson stopped by the missionaries' hotel and said, "This next location doesn't have any churches in the area, but the residents who live in that district distill and sell their own corn-based alcohol as a profession."

"Do they also drink their own corn-based alcohol as a profession?" Matthew asked.

"There are many drunkards in the area," Pastor Thompson said. "We will need to be very careful, but by the power of God's grace, I'm believing they will be set free from their bondage."

When the missionaries arrived at the outreach location, a small audience was beginning to gather around an assortment of multi-colored plastic chairs that had been arranged underneath a plantation of tall slender trees.

"We should call this location the tree-forest church," Michelle said. "It's so beautiful and peaceful here."

"These are eucalyptus trees," the Pastor said. "The landowner who is allowing us to conduct a meeting on his property plants these trees for the purpose of harvesting timber many years from now."

"What does he use the wood for?" Matthew asked.

"He sells the trees to the construction industry," the Pastor said. "Eucalyptus trees are the fastest growing trees in the world. The bark and the leaves are also useful for making natural medicine."

When the village chief arrived, Pastor Thompson gave him a warm welcome by asking the audience to extend their appreciation for his help in setting up the community meeting. After the village chief finished making all of his community-related announcements,

Matthew delivered the same message as before. He started with an overview of salvation history that's contained in the Bible, then concluded with a prayer for salvation where the audience accepted Jesus' sacrifice on the cross for the forgiveness of their sins. After encouraging the men and women to sign up for the weekly Bible study groups, Michelle was able to record eighty-three names in her notebook.

* * *

After the service ended, Draven and Thrall were able to influence a young man in tattered clothing to approach Matthew and say, "You can build a church on my mother's property. She lives down this road about three hundred meters past the junction. Please come to my house and help her. She is crippled and needs your help."

"Please allow me some time to finish greeting all the other guests," Matthew said. "Once we are finished, we can visit your home."

"It's very important that you come right away," the young man said. "My mother needs your help."

After Pastor Thompson spoke to the young man for several minutes, he said to Matthew, "You can see that this man has been drinking. He only wants you to come to his house so that you will give his mother some money. I think we should come back at a different time when he's sober to see if he's serious about donating a piece of property."

"Would it be okay if we stopped by his house to

pray with his mother?" Michelle asked.

"Everybody who lives around here knows this man is a drunkard," Pastor Thompson said. "It's important that we don't damage our reputation within the community. Let's stay focused on setting up the Bible study groups, then we can come back here tomorrow to minister to this man and his family."

11th CHAPTER

When the missionaries returned later that evening, Matthew prepared a pot of black beans and rice for dinner, along with a side dish of tomatoes and a form of sliced collard greens that the locals called *sukuma*. When the food was being served Michelle said, "My mother's Bible study group took up a collection and they are planning to send us eighteen hundred dollars."

"I was beginning to wonder how we were going to pay our hotel rent, buy school supplies for Principal Patterson, and pay Pastor Thompson for helping us with the outreach locations," Matthew said.

"It seems like every time we go somewhere, we have to buy gas and pay the driver even more money," Michelle said. "I'm wondering if we should start using motorcycle taxis to get back and forth from the Bible study groups."

"I think that would be okay," Matthew said. "I wish we could buy our own vehicle. I would like to get a Toyota Land Cruiser with a diesel engine."

"My mom's Bible study group will also send us several boxes of school supplies," Michelle said. "I gave her the address of our hotel so they could use those flat-rate international priority boxes from the post office. I think her friends were hesitant to send us money when we were ministering to the Muslims, but as soon as they found out about the schoolchildren, they became very generous."

"What are you planning to teach at the women's Bible study group?" Matthew asked.

"I'm not sure," Michelle said. "I need to spend some time in prayer with the Lord this evening so that I can put together a dynamic presentation."

* * *

Several hours before the Bible study groups were scheduled to begin, the missionaries loaded both of their daypacks with as many Bibles as would fit, then they negotiated a small fee with two motorcycle taxi drivers to transport them to the school that was located in the brick manufacturing district. When they arrived, Matthew greeted Principal Patterson in his office and asked, "Do you think we will have a good turnout this afternoon?"

"Most certainly," Principal Patterson said. "I have been inviting the parents of our students to attend the adult Bible study classes at every opportunity that has presented itself to me this week."

"Thank you for your support," Michelle said. "It's a privilege for us to be working with you."

"Many of the adults have already started to arrive," he said. "Please follow me, and I will show you to your classrooms."

Because Michelle's room was filled to capacity with eighty women, she began immediately by saying, "I wish we could provide everyone in attendance with a Kisii Bible, but for now, we will have to share because we don't have that many copies available. For those of you who have a Bible, let's start with the First Letter of Paul to the Corinthians. In chapters twelve, thirteen and fourteen, Saint Paul is describing how the Holy Spirit provides Christians with spiritual gifts so that we can use them to advance God's kingdom.

"In chapter twelve, Saint Paul starts by saying, 'Now concerning spiritual gifts, brothers and sisters, I do not want you to be uninformed.'[82] This teaching not only applies to men, but also to women, because Saint Paul doesn't want his sisters in Christ to be uninformed. He then goes on the say, 'There are varieties of gifts, but the same Spirit; and there are varieties of services, but the same Lord; and there are varieties of activities, but it is the same God who activates all of them in everyone.'[83]

"We are going to come back to this passage to study it more deeply in a minute, but for now, I wanted to point out that there are three different types of spiritual manifestations that women can use to serve the Lord. These manifestations include: spiritual gifts, services and activities.

"If you are wondering what kind of spiritual gifts

you have been given to serve the Lord, they are described in verse seven, which says, 'To each is given the manifestation of the Spirit for the common good. To one is given through the Spirit the utterance of wisdom, and to another the utterance of knowledge according to the same Spirit, to another faith by the same Spirit, to another gifts of healing by the one Spirit, to another the working of miracles, to another prophecy, to another the discernment of spirits, to another various kinds of tongues, to another the interpretation of tongues. All these are activated by one and the same Spirit, who allots to each one individually just as the Spirit chooses.'[84]

"In addition to the different types of spiritual gifts, services and activities that God has given to women for building up his church, there's also a list of leadership roles within the church that are mentioned in verse twenty-seven that says, 'Now you are the body of Christ and individually members of it. And God has appointed in the church first apostles, second prophets, third teachers; then deeds of power, then gifts of healing, forms of assistance, forms of leadership, various kinds of tongues.'[85]

"There's also the most powerful spiritual gift that's mentioned in the thirteenth chapter, which is the gift of love. We are going to go back to all these Scripture passages to study them in more detail, but for right now, they give us a good summary of the purpose of this Bible study group. It is my desire over the next several weeks to make sure that everybody in this class is an authentic follower of our Lord and Savior Jesus Christ, and that you have all received an infilling of the Holy Spirit. Once you have received the gifts of the Holy Spirit, I would like to work with you to identify your specific gifts, callings and services.

"Once you identify your own specific gifts, callings and services, I would like to help you develop those gifts, callings and services so that you can use them to advance God's kingdom here on earth."

* * *

In the men's Bible study group, Matthew was addressing a group of forty-five men and several teenage boys by saying, "In the Book of Genesis, we see the devil tempting Adam and Eve to commit the first sin.[86] In the Book of Job, we see the devil destroying a Godly man's finances, killing his family, and inflicting loathsome sores on Job from the soles of his feet to the crown of his head.[87]

"In the Gospel of Luke, we see the devil tempting Jesus. After the devil showed Jesus all the kingdoms of the world and all of their splendor, he said to him, 'To you I will give their glory and all this authority; for it has been given over to me, and I give it to anyone I please.'[88]

"In the Gospel of Luke, the devil demanded to sift Peter and the rest of the disciples like wheat.[89] In Saint Paul's letter to the Corinthians, he says that a thorn was given to him in the flesh, a messenger of Satan to torment him, to prevent him from becoming too elated.[90]

So if all these Godly men have been attacked by the devil, what makes you think that you are exempt?"

"We're not exempt," a man said. "That's why we need to know how to protect ourselves."

"There are many witch doctors in our area," another man said. "They are constantly sending curses on people who refuse to give them money for protection."

"I'm sorry to hear that," Matthew said. "The best way to protect yourselves is by putting on the full armor of God that's described in Saint Paul's letter to the Ephesians. If you want, I will share with you six simple steps that you can use to protect yourselves and your family members from the witch doctors.

"Let's begin in the sixth chapter where Saint Paul says, 'Be strong in the Lord and in the strength of his power. Put on the whole armor of God, so that you may be able to stand against the wiles of the devil. For our struggle is not against enemies of blood and flesh, but against the rulers, against the authorities, against the cosmic powers of this present darkness, against the spiritual forces of evil in the heavenly places.'[91]

"'Therefore take up the whole armor of God, so that you may be able to withstand on that evil day, and having done everything, to stand firm. Stand therefore, and fasten the belt of truth around your waist, and put on the breastplate of righteousness. As shoes for your feet put on whatever will make you ready to proclaim the gospel of peace. With all of these, take the shield of faith, with which you will be able to quench all the flaming arrows of the evil one. Take the helmet of salvation, and the sword of the Spirit, which is the word of God.'[92]

"The first step of protection is to put on the breastplate of righteousness. Because all sin is an agreement with the devil, it's not going to be possible to break free from the devil's bondage when you have one foot in the devil's kingdom and another foot in God's kingdom. Before you will be able to put on the breastplate of righteousness, you will need to denounce all of the agreements that you have made with the devil. That would include a comprehensive examination of your conscience, denouncing all your sins, denouncing all the pleasures you are receiving from your sins, and turning back to God with your whole heart. You are also going to need spiritual power from God to prevent you from committing the same sins over and over again.

"The second step of protection is to be filled with the Holy Spirit and to use your spiritual gifts to advance God's kingdom here on earth. This step is summed up in the 'shoes for our feet' or whatever makes us ready to deliver the Gospel message. Our best protection from the devil is the constant infilling of the Holy Spirit, and there's no better way to be filled with the Holy Spirit than when you're moving with the Spirit's power while advancing God's kingdom here on earth. The opposite of being filled with the Holy Spirit's power would be to fill yourself with a spirit of anger, greed or lust, and then use those sins to help the devil advance his agenda.

"The third step of protection is to practice your

spiritual affirmations. This step is summed up in the belt of truth, which should be firmly fastened around your waist, along with the shield of faith, with which you will be able to quench all the flaming arrows of the evil one. A good example of how to use your spiritual affirmations, especially when the devil throws fiery darts of negativity in your direction, is by quoting the First Letter of John that says, 'The one who is in you is greater than the one who is in the world.'[93] Let me explain that for anyone who doesn't understand: The one who dwells in your heart is the Blessed Trinity, and the *ruler of this world* is a name given to the devil, because we live in a fallen world that's under the devil's influence.[94]

"Another spiritual affirmation that I like using comes from the Book of Revelation where it says that the devil's 'time is short' and his place is in the 'lake of fire.'[95] Anytime the devil tries to throw fiery darts at me in an attempt to hinder my ministry efforts, I like using this Bible verse to remind the devil of his future.

"Another spiritual affirmation that I like using comes from the Book of Psalms, which I think everyone should memorize. That's because Psalm ninety-one says, 'You who live in the shelter of the Most High, who abide in the shadow of the Almighty, will say to the Lord, "My refuge and my fortress; my God, in whom I trust."'[96]

"'You will not fear the terror of the night, or the arrow that flies by day, or the pestilence that stalks in darkness, or the destruction that wastes at noonday. A thousand may fall at your side, ten thousand at your right hand, but it will not come near you. You will only look with your eyes and see the punishment of the wicked.'[97]

"'Because you have made the Lord your refuge, the Most High your dwelling place, no evil shall befall you, no scourge come near your tent. For he will command his angels concerning you to guard you in all your ways. On their hands they will bear you up, so that you will not dash your foot against a stone.'[98]

"The fourth step of protection is using the sword of the Spirit, which is the Word of God. We know from the Gospel of John that the devil is a liar and the father of all lies.[99] We also know that truth has the power to set people free. So when the devil tries to attack us with his lies, the best way to defend ourselves is by quoting Sacred Scripture.

"For example, when the devil tries to paralyze me with a spirit of fear, I like using the sword of the Spirit from the First Letter of John to break the bondage. That's because 'There is no fear in love, but perfect love casts out fear; for fear has to do with punishment, and whoever fears has not reached perfection in love.'[100]

"When the devil tries to hinder my ministry efforts with a spirit of negativity, I like using the sword of the Spirit from Saint Paul's letter to the Philippians that says, 'I can do all things through him who strengthens me.'[101] The Book of Romans also has a powerful verse that says,

'All things work together for good for those who love God, who are called according to his purpose.'[102]

"The fifth step of protection is using your authority in Christ to command the devil to get out of your sphere of influence. A good example of how to use your authority in Christ, which has already been given to all the Lord's disciples, comes from the life of Saint Paul. When a slave girl who was possessed by a demonic spirit of divination was interfering with his ministry efforts, he said to the spirit, '"I order you in the name of Jesus Christ to come out of her." And it came out that very hour.'[103]

"In the same way that Saint Paul commanded the demonic spirit to get out of the slave girl's life because it was interfering with his ministry efforts, you also have the ability to command demonic spirits to stop interfering with your ministry efforts."

"What happens if you command the demonic spirits to flee in Jesus' name, but they still keep interfering with you?" one man asked.

"There are several possible options to diagnose that problem," Matthew said. "The first option comes from the Acts of the Apostles when a group of Jewish exorcists tried to cast a demonic spirit out of a man using the name of Jesus. The demonic spirit said to these men, 'Jesus I know, and Paul I know; but who are you?'[104] Then the man with the demonic spirit leaped on the Jewish exorcists and overpowered them in such a way that they fled out of the house naked and wounded.

"In this situation, the Jewish exorcists had no authority in Christ because they were not authentic Christians and they were not filled with the Holy Spirit. So the first requirement for being able to drive the devil out of your life and sphere of influence is to make sure that you are an authentic, spirit-filled Christian.

"Another way to diagnose the problem is to make sure the demonic spirits that you are trying to cast out of your life are within your own sphere of influence. For example, if a demonic spirit is interfering with you, your family, business or ministry efforts, then you have the right to cast it out of your life. If your neighbor is a witch doctor, then you cannot cast a demonic spirit out of that person's life, because the witch doctor is constantly making agreements with the devil and inviting those demonic spirits into his life.

"If the witch doctor wants to denounce the devil and become a Christian, then you can help that person break free from the devil's bondage, but you cannot accept Christ on that person's behalf. The people who you are trying to help need to enter into an authentic relationship with Jesus on their own accord, and they will need to break all of their own agreements that they have made with the devil before they can be set free. You can try to help these people, but you cannot do any of the work on their behalf."

"What happens if you are an authentic Christian and the devil continues to interfere with your ministry efforts?" another man asked.

"That's when we call down the power of God," Matthew said. "The sixth step of protection is where we ask God to send his angelic army to strike down and destroy everything evil or demonic that has been interfering with your ministry efforts. We know from the Book of Hebrews that angels are ministering spirits sent to serve those who are to inherit salvation.[105]

"We also know from the Gospel of Matthew that even small children have several guardian angels that have been assigned to stand guard over them. These angels are continually beholding the face of our Father in heaven.[106] We also know from the Book of Joshua that Jesus is the Commander of the angelic army. We know this because when Joshua fell down to worship a heavenly being, the Commander of the angelic army accepted his worship, whereas angels do not accept worship or prayer requests from humans.[107]

"For example, when the Apostle John tried to worship the angel who gave him the visions in the Book of Revelation, the angel said to him, 'You must not do that! I am a fellow servant with you and your comrades the prophets, and with those who keep the words of this book. Worship God!'[108]

"So to answer your question about what we can do when demonic spirits continue to interfere with our ministry efforts, we simply pray to Jesus, the Commander of the angelic army, and ask him to send an assignment of warring angels to strike down and destroy everything evil or demonic in, on or around us, especially those entities that have been interfering with our ministry efforts. If you want, we can pray that prayer right now."

After a moment of silence where every man closed his eyes and bowed his head toward the ground, Matthew said, "Dear Lord, Jesus Christ, we come before you sinful and in great need of your assistance. Please send an assignment of warring angels to strike down and destroy everything evil or demonic in, on or around us. We ask that your warring angels butcher every demonic spirit that has been attacking us or interfering with our ministry efforts. Please destroy the entire principality where those evil spirits came from, and seal their remains in the lake of fire so that they may never again interfere with us or any other creature in the entire world ever again."

As soon as the men prayed this prayer together, Overwatch sent an assignment of angels to strike down and destroy Bloodhoof's entire principality. Over one hundred thousand angelic warriors descended upon the region with their swords drawn and ready for battle. They started their assault by cutting Draven and Thrall into pieces and continued by cutting up every other demonic spirit in the area.

After Draven and Thrall had been destroyed, the angelic warriors started hunting down and destroying all the demonic spirits that the witch doctors had sent against the Christians who were living in the area. The battle lasted more than an hour because the demonic spirits tried to flee into the abyss. After they had all been destroyed, there was a tremendous amount of spiritual peace and tranquility that settled over the region.

* * *

After Matthew finished teaching the men how to put on the full armor of God, he said, "Please come back next Saturday and bring along some friends and neighbors so that our community can continue to grow. I would like to let you guys keep the Bibles that you were using today, but we need them for another study group."

"Thank you for teaching us how to protect ourselves from the witch doctor," one man said. "I feel so much better after we prayed together."

"It was my pleasure," Matthew said. "I look forward to sharing more of God's Word with you next week."

After Matthew collected all the Bibles, Principal Patterson led the men in a closing prayer. As the men were leaving, everybody expressed a generous amount of appreciation on their way out.

* * *

After the end of a very long day, the missionaries started walking down a dusty dirt road located in front of the school as they looked around for a ride back to the hotel.

"Are you okay with hiring two motorbikes to take us back to the hotel, or would you rather ride in a car?" Matthew asked.

"While I'm sure we look funny flying around on the backs of those bikes with our daypacks stuffed full of Bibles, it's kind of fun, and I like the feeling," Michelle said. "The bikes are so much faster than a car on these rough roads, plus it provides more of an open-air experience."

"What do you mean by open air?" Matthew asked.

"When we're riding in the car, you don't get to see the wide open sky and the tops of the trees," Michelle said. "When I'm riding on the back of a bike, I feel more connected to the environment and the community."

"I never thought of it like that," Matthew said, "but you're right, it is kind of fun."

12th CHAPTER

After the missionaries spent the rest of the week setting up several more outreach locations, they loaded their daypacks full of Bibles and headed back to Principal Patterson's school for another Bible study class. Because there were so many women present in Michelle's class, she needed to move the meeting outdoors underneath the shade of an acacia tree that was growing in the courtyard.

Matthew's class had also grown in size, but because all the men still fit inside the classroom, he began by saying, "This week I was conducting a word search using my Bible software program. I found over a hundred Scripture passages that used the terms *eternity* and *eternal life*. For example, in the Gospel of Mark, a rich man approached Jesus and said, 'What must I do to inherit eternal life?'[109]

"Jesus responded with a list of commandments by saying, 'You shall not murder; You shall not commit adultery; You shall not steal; You shall not bear false witness; You shall not defraud; Honor your father and mother.'[110]

"The man responded by saying, 'I have kept all these since my youth.'[111]

"Jesus looked at him with love and said, '"You lack one thing; go, sell what you own, and give the money to the poor, and you will have treasure in heaven; then come, follow me." When he heard this, he was shocked and went away grieving, for he had many possessions.'[112]

"On the surface, this may not seem to be a very loving response, but if you look closely at the text, the Bible says that Jesus 'loved him.'[113] So to demonstrate how deeply Jesus loved this man, I brought a rope as an example. I was able to borrow it from the hardware store in Kisii Town."

After Matthew pulled a long, white rope out of his daypack, he took one end and threw it outside the classroom door. He held up the other end and said, "I want you to imagine this rope going on forever because it represents the length of time in eternity. Because eternity never ends, I want you to picture this rope extending across the nation of Kenya; and after it makes several revolutions around the world, it will continue to travel into outer space, where it will continue for all eternity without ever coming to an end.

"Now I would like you to focus your attention on this tiny black mark on the other end of the rope. Because this black mark is about one hundred centimeters long, I would like for you to imagine that it represents one hundred years of our time here on earth.

"When the rich man asked Jesus the question about eternal life, he was probably more concerned about the tiny black mark at this end of the rope, than he was about how his life on earth would affect the rest of eternity. That's why he was shocked and walked away sad. If the rich man followed the Lord's instructions—by selling his possessions and using the money to advance God's kingdom—then he would have been converting his earthly treasure into heavenly treasure.

"Because God's Word applies to every person in this room, I wanted to make sure you understand how this conversion process works. In this situation, the rich man had two choices to make: His first option would be to work very hard, save up a bunch of money for retirement, and then spend his golden years enjoying life and living off his savings. If the rich man chooses this option, he may live a nice life for the first hundred years on earth, but after that, he may be spiritually and financially bankrupt for all eternity.

"The other option for the rich man would be to follow the Lord's instructions and sell his possessions so that he could use the money to advance God's kingdom. If the rich man followed the Lord's instructions, he would need to make some sacrifices during his short time here on earth, but after that, he would have been blessed for all eternity.

"When you consider how short this black section is at the end of the rope, compared to the length of the rest of the rope that goes on for all eternity, what would be the most loving response that Jesus could have given the rich man in this situation?"

"He would have been better off selling his possessions and using the money to help the poor," a young man said who was sitting on the floor.

"Let me give you an example from my own life," Matthew said. "In the same way the rich man had two choices to make, I also have the same choices to make: I can focus my time and attention on this tiny black section of the rope, trying to save up as much money as possible in an attempt to enjoy myself during my retirement years; or I can spend my money buying Bibles and building churches so that I can be wealthy in heaven for all eternity. If Michelle and I follow the Lord's advice that's contained in Sacred Scripture, we may have to make a lot of sacrifices during the next several decades, but just think how blessed we will be for all eternity.

"I'm sharing this example with you because there's no better eternal investment opportunity than buying your own Kisii or Swahili Bible for eight hundred and fifty shillings. I know that's a lot of money for many of you, but it's the best price we could negotiate with the Kenya Bible Society.

"I would like to give every person in this room a free Bible because it would be a great way for me to convert my earthly resources into heavenly treasure; but I also wanted to share this investment opportunity with you, because it's equally important for you to invest in your own eternal destiny.

"Another bonus that you will experience by purchasing a copy of your own Bible is the satisfaction of spending your hard-earned money on something as valuable as God's Word. Because God's Word has unlimited eternal value, I'm sure every man in this room will receive more satisfaction knowing that you had to work very hard to buy your own Bible."

"I would like to buy two Bibles," one man said. "A Swahili Bible for myself and a Kisii Bible for my wife."

"I will bring you the money next week to purchase a Swahili version," another man said.

"I would like to propose a weekly collection so that the money can be used to help the widows and elderly acquire their own Bibles," Principal Patterson said.

"That's an excellent idea," Matthew said. "Because everybody in this room needs a copy of God's Word, I would like to conclude our meeting in prayer. Let's ask the Lord to open the windows of heaven and pour out an abundant blessing on the work of our hands, so that our finances may increase in the land a thousand fold."

After all the men bowed their heads and prayed for an abundant outpouring of God's blessing on their finances, several men stayed behind after everybody else had left to negotiate a lower price on a used Bible that Matthew had been carrying around in his daypack.

* * *

After several months had passed, the missionaries were able to set up twelve churches in the area, which were all in different stages of construction and development. Three of the churches that consisted of simple shade canopies were located near Lake Victoria. Two of the churches were located near the sugarcane factory. The other five churches that were constructed out of wooden planks and corrugated tin roofing sheets were located near the Vista View, Homa Bay, Tree Forest, Waterfall and Brick Manufacturing outreach locations.

* * *

Late one evening, when Matthew stopped by the Waterfall outreach location to pick Michelle up from her weekly Bible study group, he was confronted by a group of women who wanted to ask him a question.

"I would be happy to answer your questions," Matthew said to the group of thirty-two women who were seated inside the newly constructed building.

"It all started when we were studying the birth of Christ," Michelle said. "The Bible passage that we were studying came from the Gospel of Matthew where it says, 'When his mother Mary had been engaged to Joseph, but before they lived together, she was found to be with child from the Holy Spirit.'[114]

"After our conversation got sidetracked, one of the women asked me why I had been engaged for so long and why I'm still not married. Because I didn't know how to answer her question, we started talking about the marriage and engagement process in Kenya.

"In previous generations, the parents of the groom would start looking for a bride for their son. After the family paid a bride-price, the couple was married a few weeks later. In modern-day weddings, the young man and woman first need to agree to be married, and then the family of the groom will visit the bride's house to negotiate a dowry. Some families accept cows, other families accept sheep or goats, but the wealthy families only want cash.

"The bride-price is usually determined by the woman's value. If she is educated and employed or operates her own business, then she is more valuable; therefore, the family of the groom would need to pay a higher bride-price."

"I was thinking of sending Michelle's mother some backyard chickens," Matthew said. "Even though a hen can lay two hundred and fifty eggs per year, I hear they are very destructive to the landscaping and would probably tear apart her rose gardens."

Because all the women in the group remained silent with a serious look of concern on their faces, Matthew said, "You are right, I have been neglecting my fiancée. I'm not sure what to say about this, except when we first came to Kenya, we didn't know how long we would be staying. At first, we thought it would be a short-term mission trip, and then we would return home after three months to get married.

"To make matters more complicated, ever since Michelle was a little girl, she has always envisioned a beach wedding, and I have always wanted a more traditional church wedding. After we met Pastor Thompson and started conducting outreaches in the area, Michelle fell in love with the natural beauty of the countryside and with the warm hospitality of the Kenyan people.

"Before long, we were so busy conducting out-reaches, Bible study groups and building churches that I lost track of time, so... I'm very sorry, Michelle. Will you please forgive me?"

After Matthew wrapped his arms around Michelle and kissed her, the entire Bible study group erupted in excitement. It took several minutes for the women to stop clapping. When they started to calm down, Matthew continued by saying, "Because we feel at home in Kenya, and because we consider you to be our extended family, maybe we should have a Kenyan wedding."

Before Matthew could finish his proposal, the women rose to their feet and started clapping and dancing. They formed a long line, swept Michelle out of Matthew's arms and started dancing with her around the perimeter of the church.

After all the commotion settled down, Matthew continued his proposal by saying, "There's a vacation destination off the coast of Lake Victoria called Takawiri Island. It has pristine white sandy beaches, palm trees and beautiful sunsets. I'm not sure if there are any churches on the island, or if the residents who live there meet for Sunday service underneath a shade canopy or on the beach, but it would be the perfect place for a wedding."

"After spending all this time in the rural country-side, I have been thinking about a traditional wedding inside a large cathedral," Michelle said. "That way we could invite all of our friends and family members to attend."

"That sounds great," Matthew said, "except we don't have enough money to get back home."

"I'm sure Daniel and Rebecca would be happy to send us some more airline miles, so that our missionary adventures may continue..."

Notes

Excerpts from the *Catechism of the Catholic Church* are quoted from the character's memory and are based on the English translation of the *Catechism of the Catholic Church* for use in the United States of America, © 1994, United States Catholic Conference, Inc.— Libreria Editrice Vaticana. English translation of the *Catechism of the Catholic Church*: Modifications from the Editio Typica copyright © 1997, United States Catholic Conference, Inc.—Libreria Editrice Vaticana. Used with permission. All rights reserved.

Excerpts from the English translation of the Quran are quoted from the character's memory and are based on Marmaduke Pickthall's *The Meaning of the Glorious Quran*, an Explanatory Translation (New York, NY: Alfred A. Knopf, 1930). Used with permission. All rights reserved.

Interior illustrations by NightCafe Studio Art Generator. All rights reserved.

1. Kenya National Bureau of Statistics, "2019 Kenya Population and Housing Census Volume IV: Distribution of Population by Socio-Economic Characteristics," (Accessed October 1, 2023): https://www.knbs.or.ke/?wpdmpro=2019-kenya-population-and-housing-census-volume-iv-distribution-of-population-by-socio-economic-characteristics.

2. The World Bank Group, "GDP per capita (current US$)," (Accessed October 1, 2023): https://data.worldbank.org/indicator/NY.GDP.PCAP.CD.

3. Hebrews 13:4.

4. *Catechism of the Catholic Church*: 843–852 & John 14:6.

5. 1 Corinthians 9:19.

6. 1 Corinthians 9:20.

7. 1 Corinthians 9:22.

8. Acts 17:23.

9. Ibid.

10. Acts 17:28.

11. Titus 1:12.

12. 1 Corinthians 15:32.

13. The Psalms are referenced in the Quran in surahs 3:184, 4:163, 17:55, 34:10 & 35:25.

14. Revelation 3:17.

15. Noah's ark and the great flood is described in surahs 7:59–64, 10:71–73, 11:25–48, 23:23–28, 26:105–121, 54:9–16 & 71:1–28.

16. Surah 7:59.

17. Surah 11:25.

18. Surah 23:27.

19. Surah 54:16.

20. The Quran says that Jesus is the Messiah, a term used eleven times in surahs 3:45, 4:157, 4:171–172, 5:17, 5:72, 5:75 & 9:30–31.

21. Matthew 7:21–23 & Luke 6:46–49.

22. Mark 4:23, Acts 3:22–23 & Revelation 2:7.

23. John 10:27.

24. 1 Samuel 15:22, Acts 5:29 & Acts 5:32.

25. The destruction of Sodom and Gomorrah is described in surahs 7:80–84, 15:57–77, 26:160–174, 27:54–58, 29:28–35 & 37:133–138.

26. Surah 7:80.

27. Surah 15:60.

28. Surah 11:81.

29. Surah 3:156.

30. Surah 9:117, 57:9 & 59:10.

31. The Source of all Goodness in found in surah 52:28. The Protector in surahs 3:68, 7:196 & 42:28. The Loving One in surahs 11:90 & 85:14. The Provider in surah 51:58. The Bestoyer of Peace in surah 59:23. The Merciful in surahs 2:163, 3:31, 4:100, 5:98, 11:41, 12:53, 12:64, 26:9, 30:5 & 36:58. The Most Compassionate in surahs 1:3, 17:110, 19:58 & 21:112.

32. 2 Peter 3:9.

33. The Quran says that Jesus is the Messiah, a term used eleven times in surahs 3:45, 4:157, 4:171–172, 5:17, 5:72, 5:75 & 9:30–31.

34. Surah 66:12.

35. The Messiah's virgin birth is described in surahs 3:42–49, 19:16–35 & 21:91.

36. Surah 3:49.

37. Surah 5:110.

38. Luke 23:32–43 & Luke 24:13–27.

39. Jeremiah 29:11–13, Ephesians 2:10 & Philippians 1:6.

40. Luke 6:46.

41. Surah 3:19.

42. John 10:27.

43. The Quran says that Jesus is the Messiah, a term used eleven times in surahs 3:45, 4:157, 4:171–172, 5:17, 5:72, 5:75 & 9:30–31.

44. Surah 21:91.

45. The miracle of Jesus raising the dead, cleansing the lepers and healing the man born blind is described in surahs 3:49 & 5:110.

46. John 1:1–3.

47. Luke 24:17.

48. Luke 24:18.

49. Luke 24:25–27.

50. Luke 24:44–45.

51. Isaiah 53:5, Isaiah 53:7 & Isaiah 53:9.

52. Psalm 22:1.

53. Psalm 22:16 & Psalm 22:18.

54. John 1:29.

55. Exodus 12:46.

56. John 6:48.

57. John 6:51.

58. Exodus 16:4–35.

59. John 10:9.

60. Genesis 6:16.

61. John 1:51.

62. Genesis 28:12.

63. Genesis 3:8.

64. Revelation 12:4.

65. Revelation 12:7–9.

Notes

66. Jeremiah 31:31–33.
67. Luke 1:30–31.
68. Luke 1:34.
69. Luke 1:35.
70. Matthew 1:23.
71. Matthew 14:22–27 & Mark 6:35–44.
72. Matthew 8:16–17, Luke 5:12–15 & John 11:1–44.
73. Luke 24:49 & John 14:26.
74. Luke 17:7.
75. Luke 17:8–10.
76. Mark 4:3–20.
77. John 21:15–17 & Acts 20:28.
78. Matthew 25:21.
79. Matthew 28:19–20.
80. *Catechism of the Catholic Church*: 752.
81. John 10:10.
82. 1 Corinthians 12:1.
83. 1 Corinthians 12:4–6.
84. 1 Corinthians 12:7–11.
85. 1 Corinthians 12:27–28.
86. Genesis 3:1–7.
87. Job 1:6–22 & Job 2:1–7.
88. Luke 4:6.
89. Luke 22:31.
90. 2 Corinthians 12:7–9.
91. Ephesians 6:10–12.
92. Ephesians 6:13–17.
93. 1 John 4:4.
94. John 12:31, John 14:30 & John 16:11.
95. Revelation 12:12 & Revelation 20:10.
96. Psalm 91:1–2.
97. Psalm 91:5–8.
98. Psalm 91:9–12.
99. John 8:44.
100. 1 John 4:18.

Notes

101. Philippians 4:13.
102. Romans 8:28.
103. Acts 16:18.
104. Acts 19:15.
105. Hebrews 1:14.
106. Matthew 18:10.
107. Joshua 5:13–15.
108. Revelation 22:9.
109. Mark 10:17.
110. Mark 10:19.
111. Mark 10:20.
112. Mark 10:21–22.
113. Mark 10:21.
114. Matthew 1:18.

Missionaries
The Christian Social Club Adventure

Matthew Goodwin wants to move with God's power as a traveling missionary to Africa. Michelle Nobility wants to fulfill God's calling of love and marriage. Embark on a journey with the missionaries to discover how God's will is fulfilled when they encounter a presence of darkness far more sinister than they could have imagined.

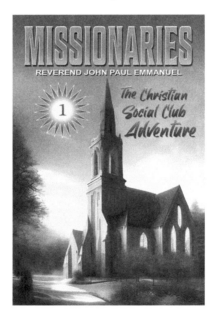

Available at your local bookstore or online.
www.ValentinePublishing.com

Missionaries
The Inner-City Homeless Adventure

The adventures of Matthew Goodwin and Michelle Nobility continue as they transition away from their Christian-singles healing ministry and into a more challenging inner-city homeless environment. In their efforts to proclaim the Gospel message to drug addicts and alcoholics, they encounter an even more sinister presence of darkness.

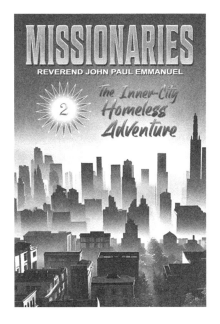

Available at your local bookstore or online.
www.ValentinePublishing.com

African Missionaries

Please consider supporting Matthew and Michelle's outreach ministry by making a tax-deductible donation to African Missionaries.

African Missionaries is a 501(c)(3) non-profit public charity that conducts mission trips to the poorest countries of the world for the purpose of spreading the Gospel message.

You can make an online donation by visiting www.ValentinePublishing.com or by sending a check to the following address:

African Missionaries
PO Box 27422
Denver, Colorado 80227

Please support our outreach ministry by distributing copies of *Missionaries, Volumes One, Two & Three* to your friends and family members.

To purchase a three-volume set,
please use the following information:

Three-Volume Set	Ministry Price
One Set	$29
Two Sets	$59
Three Sets	$89

These prices include tax and free shipping within the United States. For shipments to other countries, please contact us. Thank you for your generous support.

Please mail your payment to:

Valentine Publishing House
Missionaries — Volumes One, Two & Three
PO Box 27422
Denver, Colorado 80227